Core Collection for Small Libraries

Core Collection for Small Libraries

An Annotated Bibliography of Books for Children and Young Adults

Janice A. DeLong
and
Rachel E. Schwedt

The Scarecrow Press, Inc.
Lanham, Md., & London
1997

SCARECROW PRESS, INC.

Published in the United States of America
by Scarecrow Press, Inc.
4720 Boston Way
Lanham, Maryland 20706

4 Pleydell Gardens, Folkestone
Kent CT20 2DN, England

British Cataloguing-in-Publication Information Available

Library of Congress Cataloging-in-Publication Data

DeLong, Janice A., 1943–
    Core collection for small libraries : an annotated bibliography of books
for children and young adults / Janice A. DeLong and Rachel E. Schwedt.
        p.   cm.
    Includes bibliographical references and indexes.
    ISBN 0–8108–3252–6 (alk. paper)
    1. Children's libraries—United States—Book lists. 2. Children's stories,
English—Bibliography.   I. Schwedt, Rachel E., 1944– . II. Title.
    Z1037.D34   1997
    011.62—dc20   96–42267

ISBN 0–8108–3252–6 (cloth : alk.paper)

⊖™ The paper used in this publication meets the minimum requirements of
American National Standard for Information Sciences—Permanence of
Paper for Printed Library Materials, ANSI Z39.48–1984.
Manufactured in the United States of America.

CONTENTS

INTRODUCTION

This book was born out of need–the need for parents who want books that stress worthwhile values for their children and teachers who are trying to incorporate literature across the curriculum; the need of college students in search of books that can be used for their education class requirements; the need of young people who are hungry for a good story. As resource specialists, we had been asked numerous times for lists of books that would enhance the study of certain school subjects, yet be interesting enough to spark a child's desire to keep reading. We had also helped parents find books that expressed character qualities that would inspire young readers and encourage adolescents without being didactic.

So it was with joy that we embarked on our journey to choose books that would form the core, the essence, the "must haves" of small libraries–whether housed at home or within the walls of a school. Our audience, we hope, will be varied–perhaps the college student who was never inspired to read as a child but who has recently discovered the wonderful world of books, or the former classroom teacher who finds herself in the role of librarian in a job shift, or at the foundation of a new private or parochial school. Perhaps our reader will be a parent who has chosen the homeschool option.

Whatever your background may be, we welcome you to our core collection. Come in and browse among the shelves. You will find some familiar faces that have been around for half a century as well as some that have been named this year's best by some awards committee.

We have chosen the genre approach, that is, our chapter divisions were selected by categories such as Contemporary Fiction, Historical Fiction, Fantasy and Traditional literature. Specialty chapters, however, like Multicultural Fiction and Picture Books share a cross section of those that would traditionally be considered separate genres. Entries within each genre are arranged alphabetically by author and include title, illustrator, publisher, publication date, and suggested grade levels.

We have also included in Appendix A a list of authors you can trust for good stories with high literary quality, worthwhile character traits and interesting plots. Appendix B focuses on awards given to significant books and distinguished authors both national and international.

Finally, we wish to emphasize those features we see as unique to our book. Each annotation is followed by a list of Applications and another list of Values. These serve as guidelines for possible uses of each work. Applications make reference to the classroom subject to which the book may relate. Values reflect those character qualities demonstrated by characters in the books. Sometimes these qualities are obvious, sometimes subtle, but always thought provoking. Most importantly, we hope that the Application and Value for each book will be enjoyment. There are few pleasures that compare with opening new worlds to a child or young person through the pages of a book.

We have annotated 494 books in this collection. We would be delighted to know that you and your young person shared and enjoyed every one.

CHAPTER ONE
PICTURE BOOKS

None would question the value of the earliest possible exposure to the printed word, and picture books seem to hold special charm for the young child. Most of us have early memories that include being read to by parents, grandparents, brothers and sisters, or babysitters. Whether the volume was small enough to be carried in the pocket of a child or was a precious possession reserved for adults, we hold in ourselves the pictures and emotions it created.

With improvement in printing techniques and the growing market for well-illustrated texts, the popularity of picture books has expanded. Adults, as well as children, now boast of collections from the pen or brush of creators such as Ezra Jack Keats, David Macaulay, Beatrix Potter, or Rosemary Wells. Every artistic appetite can at least be tempted, if not appeased, by the varieties of media or techniques available. Running the gamut from the homespun pen and ink drawings of a family of mallards in *Make Way for Ducklings* by Robert McCloskey on through the surrealistic depictions of flying frogs in *Tuesday* by David Wiesnser or the paper collage illustrations of Ed Young in *Seven Blind Mice,* picture books cut across lines of taste, subject, and philosophy.

Since exposure to picture books is usually the child's first experience in reading, it is important that it be pleasant if the child is to choose to return to the world of literacy throughout his life. These books encourage prereading skills such as prediction and sequencing and can also introduce more sophisticated devices such as irony and understatement. Outstanding author, Mitsumasa Anno has provided us with exquisitely illustrated texts focusing on letters, numbers, or wordless stories which entertain while painlessly educating the prereader in basic concepts of reading and mathematics

Faced with this grand array of titles on one hand and a limit of time and funds to use in their selection on the other, we come to the question of standards for guiding our choice. Authorities would agree that well-written picture books (except those of the wordless style) contain an appropriate balance of text and illustration. These two components complement one another to form a union that is as pleasing to the eye as to the ear. The prose of Jane Yolen in *Owl Moon,* accompanied by the snowy landscapes of John Schoenherr, create a world of soft stillness into which the child can enter. Yolen's well-chosen text fulfills another requirement by using vocabulary appropriate to the developmental stage of the reader. Beginning on the first page, where the brightness of the moon makes the sky seem to shine and continuing to the last where father and child share a hope that flies on silent wings, the author employs simple words which still manage to challenge and expand the young reader's world.

A well-developed plot is as essential to a picture book as to any other story. Conflict draws the reader on to resolution, whether it be the danger created by Sam's inclination to talk "moonshine" in *Sam, Bangs, and Moonshine,* by Evaline Ness, or the internal struggle faced by Ira when he must decide whether to take his teddy bear to his friend Reggie's house in *Ira Sleeps Over* by Benard Waber, interest must be created and sustained. Successful picture books often touch on subjects of a serious tone with humor and tenderness. When Old Miss Nancy begins to lose her memory, her young friend Wilfred in *Wilfred Gordon McDonald Partridge,* by Mem Fox, manages to help in a funny yet touching manner. Whatever the subject matter, the story must deal with an issue that has meaning to a young child. Peter's disobedience and the consequence that follows, in *The Tale of Peter Rabbit*, by Beatrix Potter, exemplify an issue with which all children can relate. Although a rabbit, Peter becomes, in effect, any child who wrestles with issues of honesty and wisdom.

Sharing the story and pictures of a book creates a special bonding between reader and child. While adults may derive one kind of pleasure from the effort because of their own past experience, children may be stirred by the same book to explore and discover worlds that are new to them. Picture books provide the perfect vehicle for this exploration and plant in a child a lifelong love of the world of literacy. From the simplest wordless books, such as Mercer Mayer's *A Boy, a Dog, and a Frog,* to those as sophisticated and intricate as *Black and White*, by David Macaulay, these volumes entertain child and adult alike. Included in this chapter are a few selections which we think you may love.

Ackerman, Karen, *Song and Dance Man*. Illustrated by Stephen Gammell. Alfred A Knopf, 1988. (K–3) Caldecott Medal
When the grandchildren come to visit, Grandpa opens a dusty old trunk, pulls out tap shoes, a hat, and a cane, and transports them all to days gone by. Stephen Gammell transforms an attic into a magical place lit with the soft glow of family love, pride, and joy in each other.

Applications: Values:
Language Arts–Creative writing   Family unity
  focusing on grandparents,
  Dramatization
Psychology–Cross–generational
  relations, Role playing

Alexander, Martha (author and illustrator), *Nobody Asked Me If I Wanted a Baby Sister*. Dial Press, 1971. (K–4)
A little boy resents his new baby sister because of the attention being focused on her. It is not until he tries to give her away that he learns how important they are to each other. This is a pocket-sized book with simple words for beginning readers.

Applications: Values:
Psychology–Sibling Rivalry   Family unity
Language Arts–Dramatization   Security
Art–Draw younger siblings

Allard, Harry, *Miss Nelson Has a Field Day*. Illustrated by James Marshall. Houghton Mifflin, 1985. (1–3)
The entire Horace B. Smedley School is depressed because the football team has won no games. Miss Nelson works out a solution with a new coach, "Miss Swamp," to improve the team's performance.

Applications: Values:
Language Arts–Reading aloud   Humor,
Psychology–Problem solving   Creativity,
Sports   Team spirit

Anno, Mitsamasa (author and illustrator), *Anno's Counting Book*. Thomas Y. Crowell, 1975. (K–4)
Watercolor pictures show a landscape changing through the seasons and years as people and animals come to live there. Each page displays one-to-one relationships, groups, sets and other mathematical concepts as they appear in everyday life. Anno's books are wonderfully inventive. Other titles to enjoy include: *Anno's Alphabet, Anno's U.S.A.,* and *Topsy-Turvy.*

Applications:
Mathematics–Counting, Sets, Groups
Science–Cycle of life, Seasons

Values:
Creativity, Continuity

Bang, Molly, *Ten, Nine, Eight.* Greenwillow Books, 1983. (K–2)
Molly Bang has created a warm and fuzzy book about a little girl counting the familiar things that surround her as she is getting ready for bed. This makes a perfect bed-time story for parents to read to their children.

Applications:
Mathematics–Counting
Bedtime Stories

Values:
Security

Bluth, Brad, *Siegfried's Silent Night.* Illustrated by Toby Bluth. Children's Press, 1983.
Siegfried is a mouse whose family is living in a cathedral in Oberndorf, Austria, in 1818. As Christmas approaches and their father has not yet returned from the sea, the mice find themselves in peril, threatened with eviction by the rat landlord. While Siegfried earnestly prays for the return of his father, the family is helped by a boy who also lives in the cathedral.

Applications:
Language Arts–Reading aloud
Social Studies–Austria
Christmas

Values:
Courage, Kindness,
Faith, Ingenuity,
Cooperation

Bridwell, Norman (author and illustrator), *Clifford the Big Red Dog.* **Scholastic, 1963. (K–4)**
Clifford has become a friend of many first graders who are just learning to read. His color, size, and crazy antics make them laugh and his faithfulness to his friend Emily Elizabeth make them feel secure. What child would not enjoy being looked after by a giant red dog?

Applications: Values:
Language Arts–Easy reading   Humor, Security
Art–Drawing real or imaginary pets
Science–Pets

Brown, Marc (author and illustrator), *Arthur's Birthday.* **Little Brown, 1989. (K–4)**
Arthur and Muffy discover that they have birthdays on the same day and both are going to have a party. Instead of competing with Muffy for the loyalty of their friends, however, Arthur finds a solution that everyone can celebrate. In this entertaining series by Marc Brown, Arthur and his animal friends experience many of the situations that all children face.

Applications: Values:
Language Arts–Reading aloud,   Creativity, Humor,
  Easy reading, Introduction to
  series
Birthdays

Brown, Margaret Wise, *Goodnight Moon.* **Illustrated by Clement Hurd, Harper & Row, 1947. (K–4)**
A little bunny bids goodnight to all of the familiar things in his room and outside his window. The double-spread pictures of bunny's room gradually darkening into night and the gentle lull of the rhyming text make this a good book for helping a child settle down to sleep.

Applications: Values:
Language Arts–Bedtime stories,   Security
  Rhyming
Science–Day and night, Animals

Bunting, Eve, *Night Tree.* **Illustrated by Ted Rand. Harcourt Brace, 1991. (K–3)**
Mother, father, brother, and Nina fulfill a family Christmas tradition by finding a tree in the woods and trimming it with good things for the animals to eat. Popcorn, apples, tangerines, and balls of sunflower seeds create a lavish Christmas treat for the animals of Luke's Forest.

Applications:
Science–Conservation, Forests, Animals
Christmas

Values:
Appreciation of nature, Giving

Burningham, John (author and illustrator), *Mr. Gumpy's Outing.* **Holt, Rinehart and Winston, 1970. (K–4) Kate Greenway Medal for 1970.**
When Mr. Gumpy decides to take a ride on the river in his small boat, he is joined by children, a rabbit, a cat, a dog, a pig, and chickens, until the inevitable happens and the boat tips over. Mr. Gumpy brings the adventure to a happy conclusion, inviting them all to ride another day. Soft colors and a distinctive texture characterize this author's illustrations.

Applications:
Language Arts–Reading aloud, Dramatization

Values:
Generosity

Burton, Virginia (author and illustrator), *Mike Mulligan and His Steam Shovel.* **Houghton Mifflin, 1967. (K–4)**
After years of faithful service, Mike and his steam shovel are replaced by newer, fancier equipment. To prove that they are still useful, Mike promises to dig the cellar of the Popperville city hall in just one day. In the process, the pair make a permanent home for themselves.

Applications:
Language Arts–Compare with
  The Little Engine That Could
Social Studies–Community Helpers
Science–Machinery

Values:
Perseverance, Work ethic

Carle, Eric (author and illustrator), *The Very Hungry Caterpillar.* **Collins World, n.d. (K–4)**
Carle tells the story of the metamorphosis of this little hungry caterpillar with bold, colorful pictures. Die-cut pages show what the caterpillar eats each day of the week until he wraps himself in a cocoon, and finally emerges on the last page as a bright, beautiful butterfly.

Applications:
Mathematics–Counting, Sets,
   Days of the week
Art–Colors
Health–Nutrition
Science–Insects, Metamorphosis

Values:
Self-realization

Caudill, Rebecca, *A Pocketful of Cricket.* **Illustrated by Evaline Ness. Holt, Rinehart & Winston, 1964. (K–4)**
Jay, a young farm boy, loves the sights, sounds, and simple pleasures of his world, but most of all he loves his pet cricket. On his first day of school, Jay takes the cricket to school, where an understanding teacher helps him share his special joy with the rest of the class.

Applications:
Social Studies–Farm life
Science–Insects, Spring

Values:
Contentment, Patience

Colson, Charles, *Being Good Isn't Easy.* **Illustrated by Gwen Connelly, David C. Cook, 1986. (K–4)**
In one of a series of books designed to help children who find themselves in difficult situations make choices based on positive values, Colson tells how Allen resists the temptation to steal an apple from his neighbor's tree. Other books in the series include: *Trouble in the Schoolyard, Guess Who's at My Party,* and *Watch Out for Becky.*

Applications:
Language Arts–Reading aloud
Psychology–Decision making

Values:
Honesty, Obedience

Cosgrove, Stephen, *Fiddler*. Illustrated by Wendy Edelson. Multnomah Press, 1987. (2–12)
A mysterious bear by the name of Fiddler comes to the Land of Barely There, only to find the bears living shut up in their houses, afraid to share their goods, their talents, and their friendship. Enticing them with his melodious music and the promise of a gift more valuable than gold, Fiddler helps them to open their doors, their lives, and their hearts. Other titles in the Land of Barely There series include *Shadow Chaser, Gossamer, Derby Downs, T. J. Flopp*, and *Ira Wordworthy*.

Applications:
Language Arts–Reading aloud,
  Recreational reading
Science–Bears

Values:
Cooperation, Sharing,
Trust, Unselfishness

Crews, Donald (author and illustrator), *Freight Train*. Puffin Books, 1978. (K–3) Caldecott Honor Book
Prepositional phrases comprise most of the text of this picture book, while Crews uses primary colors as well as black and white to indicate motion and other facets of a train's life. Vivid illustrations make this a memorable book for the primary child or the beginning art student. Young children might also enjoy letting the author take them to school and home again in *School Bus*.

Applications:
Language Arts–Reading aloud
Art–Colors, Line and motion
Social Studies–Transportation

Values:
Appreciation of art
techniques

Crowther, Robert, *The Most Amazing Hide-and-Seek Alphabet Book*. Viking Press, 1977. (K–2)
Crowther has drawn an alphabet book for the kinesthetic learner, with animals hiding on every page. To find them, the child must pull or push a paper tab, or flip over a letter to the right or left. This book is fun for parents and children to read together.

Applications:
Language Arts–Alphabet
Science–Animals

Values:
Humor

Dupasquier, Philippe (author and illustrator), *Our House on the Hill.* Viking Kestrel, 1987. (K–4)
Large, softly colored pictures show the changes that come each month to a busy young family living in the country. Smaller pictures inset on the pages chronicle the seasonal activities they pursue, from birthday celebrations to gardening to picnics in the yard. The emphasis is on family.

Applications:	Values:
Science–Seasons of the year	Family relationships, Joy
Language Arts–Prereading,	of life, Sharing
Sequencing, Wordless books	

Ets, Marie Hall (author and illustrator), *Gilberto and the Wind.* Viking Press, 1963. (K–3)
Marie Hall Ets has written a number of picture books which express an appreciation of nature. In this particular story, the unsual page color and the simple sketches effectively highlight the two main characters of the book–little Gilberto and the wind. Gilberto's Hispanic heritage makes this a useful tie-in for both science and multicultural emphasis.

Applications:	Values:
Science–Wind	Appreciation of nature,
Language Arts–Reading aloud	Cultural awareness

Feelings, Muriel, *Moja Means One.* Illustrated by Tom Feelings. Dial Press, 1971. (K–2)
Muriel Feelings introduces children to basic aspects of East African life while teaching them to count from one to ten in English and Swahili. The double-spread paintings, by her husband Tom, display artistic beauty while conveying a deep respect for the East African way of life. This couple has also written an alphabet book entitled, *Jambo Means Hello.*

Applications:	Values:
Social Studies–Africa	Cultural awareness
Mathematics–Counting	

Field, Rachel, *Prayer for a Child.* **Illustrated by Elizabeth Orton Jones. Macmillan Child Group, 1941. (K–4) Caldecott Medal**
This book is a warm and loving look at a child's life as it is placed in God's care.

Applications: Values:
Language Arts–Reading aloud   Family love, Security,
                                       Thankfulness, Faith

Fleming, Denise (author and illustrator), *In a Small, Small Pond.* **Holt, Rinehart and Winston, 1993. (K–4) Caldecott Honor Book**
Fleming uses rhyming text and bright illustrations to create a picture of pond life that even very young children can understand and enjoy. A recording of sounds from a pond played as background could be used to enhance the use of this book as a read aloud.

Applications: Values:
Language Arts–Reading aloud   Appreciation of nature
Science–Pond life, Use with
   Tuesday, or *A Boy, a Dog, and*
   a Frog
Art–Draw pond animals, Make a
   collage of pond life

Fox, Mem, *Wilfred Gordon MacDonald Partridge.* **Illustrated by Julie Vivas. Kane Miller Books, 1989. (K–4)**
Wilfred Gordon MacDonald Partridge lives next door to an old people's home and he knows all of the people who live there. When he overhears his parents saying that his favorite elderly friend, Miss Nancy Alison Delacorte Cooper, is losing her memory, he sets about to help her find it. Irresistible text and illustrations show the importance of cross-generational relationships.

Applications: Values:
Psychology–Cross-generational   Friendship
   relationships

Freeman, Don (author and illustrator), *Corduroy.* **Viking Press, 1968. (K–4)**
Corduroy, a bear who lives in the toy department of a big store, longs for a home. He is convinced that he must replace the missing button on his shoulder strap before anyone will want to buy him, but Lisa loves him the way he is. Children who love *Corduroy* may also enjoy *A Pocket for Corduroy* and *Beady Bear* by the same author.

Applications: Values:
Art–Collage using buttons,   Patience, Friendship,
   Collage of teddy bears   Self–acceptance
Social Studies–Multicultural
   stories

Gag, Wanda (author and illustrator), *The ABC Bunny.* **Coward, McCann and Geoghegen, Inc., 1933. (K–2)**
Written in 1933, Wanda Gag's story still appeals to children and adults today. The black and white lithograph illustrations support a story line of action and suspense as the bunny's inquisitive nature leads it through a day full of adventure.

Applications: Values:
Language Arts–Alphabet, Reading   Inquisitiveness
   aloud, Rhyming words
Science–Rabbits

Gag, Wanda (author and illustrator), *Millions of Cats.* **Putnam, 1977. (K–4)**
When an old man and his wife become lonely, the man sets off to find a cat to keep them company. Since he cannot bear to turn even one cat away, he returns to his wife, followed by millions of cats. Since they are unable to feed them all, the couple must decide which cat to keep. They are pleased with the choice that is made.

Applications: Values:
Language Arts–Reading aloud   Ingenuity, Humility
Science–Cats, Pets
Mathematics–Counting
Psychology–Decision making

George, William T., *Winter at Long Pond.* **Illustrated by Lindsay Barrett George. Trumpet Club, 1992. (1–3)**
This author/illustrator team has created a book designed to make children more aware of the ponds and wetlands around them. The photo-quality illustrations of winter pond life, and the simple text accomplish this goal beautifully.

Applications:
Science–Woods, Wildlife, Animals, Ponds
Christmas stories

Values:
Appreciation of nature

Goodall, John S. (author and illustrator), *Shrewbettina's Birthday.* **Harcourt, Brace, Jovanovich, 1970. (K–4)**
Without words, and with the clever use of half-pages, Mr. Goodall tells of the exciting events surrounding the birthday of Shrewbettina the mole. Though the day begins with a purse snatching, it ends with a gala party full of friends and fun. The author's delicate illustrations of the English countryside reflect the joyousness of the celebration.

Applications:
Language Arts–Wordless books
Science–Woodland animals
Birthdays

Values:
Friendship

Graham, Amanda, *Who Wants Arthur?* **Illustrated by Donna Gynell, Gareth Stevens, 1984. (K–4)**
When all the rabbits in Mrs. Humber's Pet Shop are sold, Arthur the dog tries to become a rabbit so he too will be purchased. He does the same with fish and snakes and all the other animals in the store. When he finally realizes that he might as well be an ordinary brown dog, he finds that there is someone who wants him just the way he is. Donna Gynell's illustrations are hilarious. Arthur also appears in *Always Arthur* and *Educating Arthur.*

Applications:
Science–Dogs, Pets
Psychology–Self-acceptance

Values:
Individuality, Humor

Gramatky, Hardie (author and illustrator), *Little Toot.*
G. P. Putnam, 1967. **(K–4)**
Little Toot loves his carefree life on the river making fancy figure eights while his father and the other large tugboats work hard to pull the big ocean liners into port. Then one day, when a fierce storm leaves a liner jammed between two huge rocks and Little Toot is the only one near enough to help, he discovers that there is real satisfaction in working hard to help someone else.

Applications: Values:
Language Arts–Compare to *The*   Responsibility,
   Little Engine That Could   Work Ethic
Social Studies–Transportation

Henkes, Kevin (author and illustrator), *Owen.* **Green-willow, 1993.** **(K–4)** **Caldecott Honor Book**
Anyone who has ever had a favorite blanket, will relate to Owen and his desire to have his fuzzy yellow blanket with him at all times. The author has created an endearing mouse family who finds an inventive solution to this childhood situation.

Applications: Values:
Show and Tell–Child's favorite   Family life, Security
   toy or item
Bedtime Stories
Language Arts–Compare to
   Something for Nothing

Hoban, Russell, *A Birthday for Frances.* **Illustrated by Lillian Hoban. Harper and Row, 1968.** **(K–4)**
Frances, a little badger who expresses her thoughts in song, has trouble being generous when her little sister Gloria has a birthday party. With encouragement from her parents, however, Frances finally gives up sulking and rises to the occasion.

Applications: Values:
Psychology–Sibling rivalry   Generosity, Humor
Birthdays

Hoff, Syd (author and illustrator), *Nutty Noodles.*
Scholastic Books, 1980. (K–2)
Using the letters of the alphabet as a starting point, Syd Hoff has
created pages of humorous line drawings. This simple, wordless
alphabet book sized to fit in a small child's hand, will stir children's
imagination and strengthen their powers of observation while they
learn the alphabet.

Applications:
Art–Draw own pictures
  starting with letters
Language Arts–Alphabet

Values:
Imagination

Hughes, Shirley (author and illustrator), *Alfie's Feet.*
Lothrop, Lee and Shepard Books, 1982. (K–2)
Alfie loves to walk through puddles and mud, so one day his mother
buys him a pair of shiny new yellow boots. However, something is
not quite right with Alfie's boots. They feel funny on his feet until
Dad helps to straighten them out. Hughes has illustrated this simple
story with warm, wonderful pictures of family.

Applications:
Physical Development–Left/Right
Psychology–Sibling relations,
  Family relations

Values:
Empathy, Humor

Hunt, Angela Elwell, *If I Had Long, Long Hair.* **Illus-**
trated by L. Diane Johnson. Abingdon Press, 1988. (K–4)
Loretta imagines what it would be like to have beautiful long hair that
would cascade out behind her. The longer her hair grows, however,
the more tangled her daydream becomes until Loretta decides to be
content with what she has.

Applications:
Language Arts–Reading aloud
Art–Draw something you would
  like to change about yourself
Psychology–Self-acceptance

Values:
Contentment, Humor

Keane, Glen (author and illustrator), *Adam Raccoon and the Race to Victory Mountain.* **David C. Cook, 1993.**
Adam Raccoon desperately wants to win the race to Victory Mountain, but with so many fascinating distractions, it is difficult to keep his feet on the course. It is King Aren's intervention that rescues him from defeat and helps him win his trophy.

Applications: Values:
Language Arts–Parables   Perseverance, Honesty,
Physical Education–Races   Single–mindedness

Keats, Ezra Jack (author and illustrator), *The Snowy Day.* **Viking Press.** **(K–4) Caldecott Medal**
Peter discovers the wonders of the first snowfall as he plays in the streets outside his apartment building, making paths through the crunchy snow, building a snowman, and sliding down tall drifts. The illustrations of the book are done in collage, a medium frequently employed by Keats in his stories about Peter, a young African-American boy.

Applications: Values:
Social Studies–Multicultural stories Appreciation of nature
Science–Weather, Snow
Art–Collage techniques

Kellogg, Steven, *The Island of the Skog.* **Dial Press, 1973. (K–4)**
Tired of running away from city cats and dogs, Jenny and her mouse friends set out to find a peaceful place to live. They seem to have found it until giant footprints shake their security. Steven Kellogg successfully combines humor and good sense to create a book that children will love and learn from. With each reading new details will be found in his finely drawn illustrations.

Applications: Values:
Language Arts–Dramatization   Courage, Acceptance
Psychology–Communication,
   Dealing with fear

Kraus, Robert, *Leo the Late Bloomer.* **Illustrated by Jose Aruego. E. P. Dutton, 1971.** (K–4)
What parent has not worried about the son or daughter who just does not seem to blossom like the rest of their children? Leo's father is fretting because the little lion cub is not able to do anything right. Then one day, in his own time, Leo blooms. This story offers hope to parents and late bloomers alike reminding them to be patient with each other.

Applications:
Language Arts–Reading aloud
Psychology–Late maturation
Science–Animals
Social Studies–Africa

Values:
Individuality, Patience,
Understanding

Leaf, Munro, *The Story of Ferdinand.* **Illustrated by Robert Lawson. Viking Press, 1938.** (1–3)
Unlike the other bulls, who like to butt each other and fight with their horns, Ferdinand loves to sit alone in the field and smell the flowers. When he refuses to fight in the bullfighting ring, he is taken back to the pasture in disgrace. Ferdinand, however, is not bothered at all. He is right where he wants to be.

Applications:
Psychology–Peer pressure
Social Studies–Spain, Bullfighting
Science–Animals

Values:
Individuality

Lear, Edward, *An Edward Lear Alphabet.* **Illustrated by Carol Newsome. Lothrop, Lee and Shepard, 1983.** (K–2)
Carol Newsome's whimsical little mouse ushers the reader through the illustrations drawn to accompany Edward Lear's humorous verses. The rhyming nonsense words should make children laugh as they learn their letters.

Applications:
Language Arts–Alphabet,
    Nonsense verse, Sequencing

Values:
Humor

Leodhas, Sorche Nic, *Always Room for One More.* Illustrated by Nonny Hogrogrian. Holt, Rinehart & Winston, 1965. (2–4)
Lachie MacLachlan always has room for one more stranger passing by who has need of a warm meal and a roof over his head. One day, however, his little house reaches the bursting point and his guests have opportunity to repay Lachie's kindness.

Applications: Values:
Language Arts–Rhyming   Generosity, Friendship
Mathematics–Counting
Social Studies–Scotland, Cultural
  awareness

Levison, Wendy Cheyette, *Going to Sleep on a Farm.* Illustrated by Juan Wijngaard. Dial Books, 1992. (K–1)
As his father describes how each animal on the farm goes to sleep for the night, the little boy becomes drowsier and drowsier, until he too is tucked in for the night.

Applications: Values:
Language Arts–Rhyming   Security
Science–Animals
Social Studies–Farm life
Bedtime Stories

Lionni, Leo (author and illustrator), *Frederick.* Pantheon, 1967. (K–4)
Frederick is different from the other little field mice. While they collect food for the winter, Frederick sits on a rock collecting sun rays, colors, and words. When winter stretches long, the nuts, berries, and corn begin to run low. It is then that the mice learn to appreciate the supplies that Frederick has stored.

Applications: Values:
Language Arts–Creative writing,   Sharing, Empathy,
  Poetry   Individuality
Psychology–Understanding
  differences in people

Lucado, Max, *Just in Case You Ever Wonder.* **Illustrated by Toni Goffe. Word Kids! 1992. (K–4)**
Parents having difficulty expressing love to their children could use this book by Max Lucado to do it for them. In simple but eloquent style, the author tells children how special they are by giving them a message of love, comfort, and protection.

Applications:
Bedtime Stories
Psychology–Building self-
  acceptance

Values:
Family love

Macaulay, David (author and illustrator), *Black and White.* **Houghton Mifflin, Boston, 1990. (4–6) Caldecott Medal**
Macaulay has created a mystery in a picture book, or a picture book containing a mystery, or just a mysterious picture book. Whatever it is, the reader will be intrigued by trying to put together the puzzle pieces. Macaulay uses a convict, newsprint, and a bull terrier to convince the reader that what may appear as clear-cut as black and white may not always be just that way.

Applications:
Language Arts–Creative writing,
  Compare with other Macaulay
  books
Art–A picture within a picture

Values:
Creativity

McCloskey, Robert (author and illustrator), *Make Way for Ducklings.* **Viking Press, 1976. (K–4) Caldecott Medal**
This classic picture book describes the life of a duck family in New York City. Mama lays her eggs and hatches her family near a pond in Central Park. City life goes on around the vulnerable ducklings, yet even the city policeman lends a hand to keep them safe.

Applications:
Language Arts–Reading aloud
Science–Wildlife, Ducks
Social Studies–New York City

Values:
Family unity, Security,
Kindness to animals

McCloskey, Robert (author and illustrator), *Time of Wonder.* **Viking Press, 1957.** (2–5)
A summer spent on an island in Penobscot Bay forms the backdrop for this timeless story filled with awe and joy in the world of God's creation. McCloskey pens the narrative with such beauty and grace that readers are left wondering whether they are reading poetry or prose.

Applications:
Science–Weather, Islands,
  Sea life
Social Studies–New England
Language Arts–Reading aloud

Values:
Family Unity,
Appreciation of nature

Mayer, Mercer (author and illustrator), *A Boy, a Dog and a Frog.* **Dial Press, 1967.** (K–4)
In a delightfully humorous wordless story, a little boy and his dog set out to the pond to catch a frog. The clever frog outwits them and, in a suprising twist of frog logic, becomes their friend. Mercer Mayer is a master of creating wordless books.

Applications:
Language Arts–Storytelling,
  Sequencing, Prediction
Science–Frogs, Pond Life

Values:
Creativity, Humor,
Friendship

Minarik, Else Holmelund, *Little Bear.* **Illustrated by Maurice Sendak. Harper & Row, 1957.** (K–4)
When Little Bear asks his mother for something to put on, so that he can play in the snow, she gives him a hat, a jacket, and finally snow pants. When he declares that he is still cold, she asks if he would like a fur coat and simply removes his winter clothing. Minarik has written a joyous book full of everyday adventure. First graders can read this and other Little Bear books by themselves.

Applications:
Language Arts–Easy reading
Science–Bears

Values:
Family love,
Unselfishness

Moncure, Jane Belk, *Word Bird's Shapes.* **Illustrated by Linda Hohag. Children's Press, 1983. (K–1)**
Word Bird is given boxes of paper of various shapes and colors. With each box of shapes he makes special pictures. When the boxes containing the different shapes fall, Word Bird discovers that he can make many more things when he mixes the shapes together.

Applications:
Language Arts–Vocabulary
Mathematics–Shapes
Art–Colors

Values:
Imagination

Ness, Evaline (author and illustrator), *Sam, Bangs, and Moonshine.* **Holt, Rinehart & Winston, 1966. (K–4) Caldecott Award**
Samantha, a fisherman's daughter, loves to tell strange stories, especially to her friend Thomas who believes every word she says. Her father warns her that this habit of talking "moonshine" is trouble, but Sam persists until the day her moonshine almost costs the lives of Thomas and her cat Bangs.

Applications:
Language Arts–Reading aloud
Psychology–Single parenting
Science–Storms
Social Studies–New England

Values:
Honesty, Friendship

Nichols, Roy and Doris. *I'm No Ordinary Chicken.* **Illustrated by Paul Mangold. Sweet Publishing, 1987.**
Hattie believes that she is braver, smarter, and prettier than the other chickens who live in Farmer Schult's henhouse, so she sets off to Farmer Yoder's barnyard where she is sure life is more exciting. The hens there soon make her realize what a good life she had already. When her owner comes to claim her, she returns with a thankful heart.

Applications:
Social Studies–Rural life
Science–Chickens

Values:
Humility, Thankfulness

Peet, Bill (author and illustrator), *Zella, Zack and Zodiac.*
Houghton Mifflin, 1986. (1–4)
Zella the zebra rescues Zack the ostrich chick when it is left behind
by the other ostriches. When Zella's baby Zodiac is attacked by a
lion, Zack the ostrich returns the rescue. With humorous drawings
and verse, Peet teaches lessons of loyalty and friendship.

Applications: Values:
Language Arts–Rhyme   Friendship, Loyalty,
Science–Animals   Gratitude, Friendship
Social Studies–Africa

Piper, Watty, *The Little Engine That Could.* **Illustrated by**
George and Doris Hauman. Platt & Munk, 1990.
When the bigger engines refuse to carry a train of toys and food to
children in a distant city, the little blue engine volunteers to pull the
freight cars over the mountainous route. The little engine's determination compensates for its lack of size.

Applications: Values:
Language Arts–Compare to *Mike*   Charity, Diligence,
  Mulligan and His Steam Shovel   Perseverance
Art–Use construction paper cut-
  outs to create a train
Social Studies–Transportation

Potter, Beatrix (author and illustrator), *The Tale of Peter*
Rabbit. **F. Warne & Co., 1902.**
Peter Rabbit is the first and most famous of the author's menagerie
of twenty-three animal characters. He is perhaps the most loved
rabbit in all of children's literature. The adventures of this precocious
bunny in Mr. McGregor's garden excite and amuse children and
adults alike. The pocket-sized editions published by F. Warne & Co.
are just the right size for little hands.

Applications: Values:
Language Arts–Reading aloud   Obedience
Science–Rabbits, Gardening

Rey, H. A. (author and illustrator), *Curious George Rides a Bike.* **Houghton Mifflin, 1952. (K–4)**
The mischievous antics of this wide-awake little monkey take him in and out of trouble. This series of books about adventures brought about by George's curiosity will delight young readers.

Applications:
Science–Monkeys
Language Arts–Prediction

Values:
Responsibility, Humor, Individuality, Forgiveness

Scarry, Richard (author and illustrator), *Richard Scarry's Best Story Book Ever.* **Western Publishing, 1950. (K–4)**
Richard Scarry is one of the best-selling author/illustrators in children's literature. His humorous tales have been translated into twenty-eight languages. Using animals as subjects, he is able to combine instruction with marvelous entertainment.

Applications:
Language Arts–Reading aloud, Vocabulary
Mathematics–Counting
Social Studies–Transportation
Science–Seasons

Values:
Manners, Obedience
Courtesy, Helpfulness

Scholey, Arthur. *Baboushka: a Traditional Russian Folk Tale.* **Illustrated by Ray and Corinne Burrows, Crossway Books, 1977. (K–3)**
Baboushka, busily occupied keeping the cleanest house in the town, does not seriously consider the bright star which appears in the heavens over her village. Even when three strangers who are following this star invite her to accompany them on their journey, she feels bound by her household duties. Later, when she does decide to follow, she is too late to see the treasure that the star was sent to reveal.

Applications:
Language Arts–Folk stories
Social Studies–Russia
Christmas stories

Values:
Keeping right priorities

Dr. Seuss (Theodor Geisel, author and illustrator), *Horton Hatches the Egg.* **Random House, 1940.** **(K–4)**
Horton the elephant suffers through many dangers, discomforts and indignities, remaining faithful to his promise to protect the egg of Mazie, a lazy, irresponsible bird. While the elephant is sitting on Mazie's egg, she is warming her feathers on southern beaches. In the end, Horton's faithfulness is justly rewarded. Horton is one of numerous characters created by Theodor Geisel which delight, entertain, and encourage the young to read.

Applications:
Language Arts–Reading
aloud, Prereading,
Predicting
Science–Animals

Values:
Faithfulness, Responsibility,
Perseverance, Humor,
Friendship

Sharmat, Marjorie Weinman, *Twitchell the Wishful.* **Illustrated by Janet Stearns. Holiday House, 1981.** **(1–3)**
Twitchell Mouse is envious of the belongings of all of his friends and cannot resist telling them how he wishes that their things belonged to him. When his friends generously give him everything he wants, Twitchell discovers that he is happiest with his own things after all. The detailed sketches of Janet Stevens add much delight and humor to the story.

Applications:
Language Arts–Reading
aloud, Dramatization

Values:
Contentment, Friendship

Shulevitz, Uri (author and illustrator), *Rain, Rain, Rivers.* **Farrar, Straus and Giroux, 1969.** **(K–2)**
Shulevitz has written a lyrical tribute to rain that patters on the roofs of houses, swells the ocean waves, and creates "pieces of sky" in the street for children to jump over. This is an exuberant work in which words and pictures come together in celebrating nature.

Applications:
Science–Weather, Water

Values:
Appreciation of nature

Steig, William (author and illustrator), *Sylvester and the Magic Pebble.* **Simon & Schuster, 1969. (K–4)**
After finding a magic pebble that will grant people's wishes, Sylvester meets a lion and, in his panic to escape, wishes himself to be a stone. Sylvester's sad parents unknowingly find the pebble and place it on the stone where he is able to wish himself real again. Emphasis is on the importance of family love over material possessions.

Applications:
Psychology–Fear, Decision
making
Language Arts–Reading aloud

Values:
Family life, Wisdom

Tresselt, Alvin, *Hide and Seek Fog.* **Illustrated by Roger Duvoisin. Lothrop, Lee & Shepard, 1965. (K–2)**
Pictures and words combine to make the reader feel the chill, dampness, and mystery of a New England fog as it rolls in from the sea, sending vacationers and natives alike back to their docks and cottages. This is the same author/illustrator combination that produced the Caldecott Winner *White Snow, Bright Snow.*

Applications:
Social Studies–Cape Cod
Science–Weather, Seashore,
Fog

Values:
Appreciation of nature

Viorst, Judith, *Alexander and the Terrible, Horrible, No Good, Very Bad Day.* **Illustrated by Ray Cruz. Atheneum, 1978. (K–4)**
It is hard to imagine that anything else could have gone wrong for Alexander on this particular day. It is disaster from morning to evening. Anyone who has had a bad day can certainly sympathize with him and enjoy a wry chuckle or two.

Applications:
Language Arts–Reading aloud
Art–Draw pictures of a bad day
which you have had

Values:
Humor, Attitude

Waber, Bernard (author and illustrator) *Ira Sleeps Over.*
Houghton Mifflin, 1972. (K–2)
Ira is looking forward to staying overnight at Reggie's house. They
plan a great agenda including a wrestling match, a pillow fight,
checkers, and dominoes. Ira just has one question: Should he take
his teddy bear along? Everyone gives him different advice, but
Reggie finally provides the answer.

Applications: Values:
Language Arts–Reading aloud   Self-acceptance, Humor
Psychology–Problem solving,
   Peer pressure

Waite, Michael P., *Casey the Greedy Young Cowboy.*
Illustrated by Anthony De Rosa. David C. Cook, 1988.
(K–4)
Cowboy Casey is unhappy when his parents will not buy him all of
the western gear that he wants. When he meets Bronco Bill, who has
all the cowboy trappings he wants but does not have a family who
loves him, young Casey begins to realize the value of what he has.
Casey is one character from a series of books by Michael Waite called
Building Christian Character.

Applications: Values:
Language Arts–Reading aloud,   Thankfulness
   Poetry, Dramatization

Ward, Lynd (author and illustrator), *The Biggest Bear.*
Houghton Mifflin, 1952. (K–4) Caldecott Medal
Johnny Orchard is humiliated because almost all the barns in the
valley have bearskins nailed up to dry, except theirs. When he sets
out to redeem his family's honor, he brings home more than his
family or his neighbors can handle. Finding a solution is more
difficult than Johnny first imagined.

Applications: Values:
Language Arts–Prereading,   Responsibility, Pride
   Prediction
Science–Animal care, Bears

Wells, Rosemary, *Forest of Dreams*. Illustrated by Susan Jeffers. Dial Books for Young Readers, 1988.
The poetic text of Rosemary Wells celebrates the seasons of the earth, giving thanks to the Creator for life and the ability to enjoy the beauty of nature. Supported by the soft, sensitive oil paintings of Susan Jeffers, this book will delight and inspire the reader.

Applications: Values:
Language Arts–Reading aloud   Appreciation of nature
Science–Seasons, Forest,
  Senses

Wiesner, David (author and illustrator), *Tuesday*. Clarion Books, 1991. (K–4) Caldecott Medal
In this nearly wordless book of nonsense, frogs rise from the pond and spend the night floating through the sleeping town on their lily pads. Together they watch television, chase dogs, and get caught in washing that is hanging on the line. When morning comes, the evidence of their nighttime activity leaves puzzled residents wondering what had happened.

Applications: Values:
Language Arts–Prereading,   Humor
  Prediction
Science–Frogs

Williams, Vera (author and illustrator), *Three Days on a River in a Red Canoe*. Mulberry Books, 1981. (2–5)
When a little girl sees a red canoe for sale in a neighbor's yard, it marks the beginning of a great adventure. Readers are allowed to share the planning, the work, and the fun of a three-day canoe trip taken by Mother, Aunt Rosie, and the two children. Waterfalls, storms, and wild animals all add to the excitement of the trip.

Applications: Values:
Language Arts–Journaling   Cooperation, Planning,
Science–Wildlife, Weather,   Family unity
  Canoes, Camping
Art– Draw pictures of a vacation

Wood, A. J., *LOOK! The Ultimate Spot-the-Difference Book.* Illustrated by April Wilson. Penguin Books, 1990. (K–4)
Pages that look identical have subtle but vital differences. Each one displays the wonders of nature in such diverse places as the African savanna, Japan's volcanic mountains and the depths of the Red Sea. This book makes an excellent discussion starter.

Applications: Values:
Language Arts–Research   Animal Appreciation,
Music–Share the music of different   Art appreciation
  geographic areas
Science–Habitats
Social Studies–Geography

Yolen, Jane, *Owl Moon.* Illustrated by John Schoenhorr. Philomel, 1987. (K–4) Caldecott Medal
This poetic story of a young child's first experience owling with her father is beautifully complemented by John Schoenherr's soft watercolors. One can feel the cold stillness, the special companionship, and the anticipation of the winter night.

Applications: Values:
Science–Birds, Owls   Appreciation of nature,
Bedtime stories   Family unity, Tradition

Young, Ed (author and illustrator), *Seven Blind Mice.* Philomel Books, 1992. (K–4)
Seven blind mice investigate a strange Something that comes to their pond. As children join in their investigation they can explore colors, numbers, days of the week, and various sensory experiences. It is only when all the mice put their experiences together that they learn the truth.

Applications: Values:
Language Arts–Dramatization   Cooperating,
Art–Colors   Considering the whole
Mathematics–Numbers   picture
Science–Days of the week

Zolotow, Charlotte, *William's Doll*. Illustrated by William Pene Du Bois. Harper & Row, 1972. (K–4)
When William wants a doll, his brother says he is creepy. His father buys him a basketball and the neighbor calls him "sissy." Grandma understands that he just wants something to love, so that he can practice being a father.

Applications:
Language Arts–Creative writing
Art–Draw your favorite toy
Psychology–Peer pressure

Values:
Individuality, Parenting skills

CHAPTER TWO
TRADITIONAL LITERATURE

"Did I ever tell you about the time Grandpa . . .?" So begins one of the most personal and memorable means of transmitting culture from one generation to the next. When this process is repeated from generation to generation for several hundred years, we have a firmly established oral tradition. The combination of passing down family and community stories by word of mouth and the eventual canonization of such stories results in a genre designated as traditional literature, folk literature, or folklore. Individual members of this broad literary family include folk tales, fairy tales, myths, legends, fables, and tall tales. Some authorities include Mother Goose rhymes (having no known author) and folk songs. Others disagree whether to include the literary fairy tales (those with a known author) in this family or with other fantasy literature. We will list all fairy tales under this division since children are generally indifferent to authorship and the applications are essentially the same.

Well known sources of folk literature that have greatly influenced English-speaking cultures come to us from France, Germany, and Denmark. Charles Perrault compiled a volume of French stories in 1697 which has reached down through the centuries to touch thousands of readers. The popularity of some of the selections from that book is evident three hundred years later, as we continue to enjoy "Cinderella," "Little Red Riding Hood," and "Puss in Boots."

During the nineteenth century, two brothers, Jacob and Wilhelm Grimm, set out to research the history, customs, and language of their native Germany by traveling around the countryside asking people to tell stories they could remember from the past. This written form of oral history reveals the values and soul of the people as no history book could. Although they made contributions to the archives of their home country as planned, they are best known around the world for *Grimm's Fairy Tales,* a product of their interviews. Originally written for adults, children's adaptations have become favorites of both young and old. The many editions of Grimm's stories that have been illustrated by well-known contemporary illustrators attest to their popularity.

Hans Christian Andersen represents another major branch on the folklore family tree. Growing up in Denmark, Andersen tried several forms of writing as well as acting when he ventured out on his own. He nearly starved before finding that his talent lay in writing fairy tales. Fortunately, he soon became successful and was well received by his countrymen, including those peers who had rejected him as a child, an experience which was reflected in his autobiographical story "The Ugly Duckling." Other popular stories by Andersen that contain timeless lessons for life are "The Emperor's New Clothes" and "The Nightingale." These and many others are included in this chapter in Andersen's *Fairy Tales.*

In our recommended list, we include folktales from many countries and a variety of ethnic groups because we feel that comparison, contrast, and compassion are essential elements of survival to citizens teetering on the brink of the twenty-first century. Children also need to recognize and respect their own cultural heritage. Studying the legacy of their nation's folklore enriches children's understanding of their own past.

As our society becomes more mobile and the world seems to be shrinking, we will be faced with many more opportunities to share cultural diversity. Values, customs, religion, and sense of humor of ethnic groups may be glimpsed through reading folk literature. Children need heart knowledge as well as head knowledge of those who differ from them in skin color, religion, heritage, or region.

Our list is not exhaustive, and the field is extensive. We have simply tried to include representative samples that will increase the reader's or listener's desire for more.

Aardema, Verna (adapter), *Why Mosquitos Buzz in People's Ears.* **Illustrated by Leo and Diane Dillon. Dial Press, 1975. (K–4) Caldecott Award**
When the Sun is not awakened by Mother Owl, King Lion calls for a council meeting of his subjects. As each animal blames the other, a flashback sequence is formed. Similarities to the familiar game of Gossip will demonstrate to children that misunderstandings can often be averted by returning to the source. Dramatic art work accompanies the text.

Applications: Values:
Social Studies–Africa   Courage, Honesty,
Language Arts–Storytelling,   Taking responsibility
Dramatization

Aesop (trans. by V. S. Vernon Jones), *Aesop's Fables.* **Illus. by Arthur Rackham. Avenel Books, 1912. (K–12)**
The observations of Aesop have been recognized for their wisdom for more than 2000 years. These brief anecdotes, generally using animals as subjects, express wisdom through common events and would be a good source for the beginning storyteller. Most have a lesson or moral as a concluding line.

Applications: Values:
Language Arts–Reading aloud,   Wisdom, Humor,
  Dramatization, Create own fables   Many virtues

Alexander, Lloyd, *The Fortune Tellers.* **Illustrated by Trina Schart Hyman. Dutton, 1992. (5–8)**
Lively, humorous illustrations enhance this tongue-in-cheek folktale. By a twist of fate, the seeker becomes the seer and we all see how fortune tellers, too, have limited vision.

Applications: Values:
Social Studies–Cameroon   Humor,
Language Arts–Dramatization,   Cultural awareness
  Example of trickster tale
Art–Aesthetic value of detailed pictures

Andersen, Hans Christian, *Fairy Tales.* **Illus. by Arthur Rackham. Weathervane Books, 1932.** **(K–8)**
Rackham's illustrations lend an old-fashioned air of dignity and grace, as well as mischief, to this beloved collection of literary fairy tales. Andersen's stories magnify the good and encourage the faint of heart.

Applications: Values:
Language Arts–Reading aloud,   Courage, Perseverance,
  Storytelling, Creative writing   Unselfishness
Social Studies–Denmark

Andersen, Hans Christian, *The Ugly Duckling.* **Retold and illus. by Troy Howell, G.P. Putnam & Sons, 1990.** **(K–8)**
This is a beautifully illustrated version of the less-than-beautiful child blossoming into a lovely and successful adult. The main characters may be swans, but the message of patience is there for parents and children as well.

Applications: Values:
Language Arts–Reading aloud,   Patience, Love,
  Recreational reading   Self-Acceptance
Science–Ducks, Swans
Psychology–Self concept,
  Late bloomers

Bang, Molly, *The Paper Crane.* **Greenwillow, 1985.** **(K–4)**
Molly Bang's seemingly three-dimensional collage and origami illustrations create a lifelike quality in this Japanese folktale. The generosity of a poor restaurant owner to a penniless stranger results in prosperity for both through the magic of a paper crane.

Applications: Values:
Art–Collage or origami   Generosity, Creativity
Social Studies–Japan
Language Arts–Reading aloud,
  Dramatization
Music–Accompany story with
  Japanese instruments

Balian, Lorna, *Leprechauns Never Lie.* **Parthenon Press, 1987. (K–8)**
Humor and the value of hard work form the basis of this Irish folktale. Ninny Nanny is a lazy child but accomplishes her chores with determination when on the trail of a wee man's treasure.

Applications: Values:
Language Arts–Folklore,   Work Ethic, Humor,
   Dramatization   Perseverance
Social Studies–Ireland

Bierhorst, John (compiler), *Doctor Coyote: A Native American Aesop's Fables.* **Illustrated by Wendy Watson,. Macmillan Publishing Company, 1987. (K–8)**
Bierhorst has collected twenty fables featuring Coyote as the trickster/main character. Each story is less than one page in length and ends with a moral. Represented are legends of the Aztecs, loosely following the format of Aesop.

Applications: Values:
Language Arts–Storytelling,   Cultural awareness,
   Retelling in Spanish   Lessons taught in
Social Studies–Aztec Indians   each story
Compare to *Aesop's Fables*

Bierhorst, John (compiler), *The Mythology of North America.* **William Morrow, 1985. (5–12)**
Bierhorst gives background and setting to the mythology that grew out of the Native American tribes. The introduction includes information about researchers from the 1800s and their collective contribution to knowledge of early American culture. Maps and descriptions of motifs grouped by geographical area make the book an invaluable tool for teacher or folklorist.

Applications: Values:
Language Arts–Study of motifs   Cultural awareness,
   related to the culture   Morality as demon-
Social Studies–Research on tribes strated by tribes

Bierhorst, John (editor), *The Ring in the Prairie.* **Illus. by Leo and Diane Dillon. Dial Press, 1970.** (5–12)
This Swanee legend is reminiscent of the "Twelve Dancing Princesses," yet with a distinctively Native American flavor. At the conclusion of the story, both mortal and immortal experience transformation.

Applications:
Language Arts–Compare to other
  transformational tales,
  Storytelling
Science–Ecology

Values:
Cultural awareness

Blair, Walter (compiler), *Tall Tale America.* **Illus. by Glen Rounds. Coward-McCann, 1944.** (5–12)
This tall tale collection covers all geographic areas of America. Some heroes of these extraordinary epics are Captain Stormalong, Jonathan Slick, Daniel Boone, Mike Fink, and Paul Bunyan. Timelessness of topic makes these stories just as much fun in contemporary times as when they were first told.

Applications:
Language Arts–Storytelling,
  Creative writing
Social Studies–Regional heroes

Values:
Humor, Creativity

Brett, Jan (adapter and illustrator), *Beauty and the Beast.* **Trumpet Book Club, 1989.** (4–9)
This beautifully illustrated story of a daughter's love for her father and sacrifice for her family is memorable indeed. Brett has used delightful foreshadowing techniques in her elaborate artwork that are worth the price of the book. The lesson of not judging by appearances is made quite clear in this version of the well-known tale.

Applications:
Language Arts–Reading aloud,
  Comparison with other versions
  in both written word and video

Values:
Loyalty, Courage,
Sacrifice, Recognizing
prejudice

Brett, Jan, *Goldilocks and the Three Bears*. Retold and illus. by Jan Brett. Dodd, Mead & Co., 1987. (K–2)
Never has the Bear family been more appealing as in this intricately illustrated version of the familiar story. Although an interloper, Goldilocks is portrayed as a beautiful child, full of curiosity as she explores the exquisitely decorated Bear home. Bordered pages provide yet a third dimension of artistic design in this sure-to-be-a-favorite book.

Applications: Values:
Language Arts–Reading aloud,   Family unity
  Storytelling, Dramatization

Bruchac, Joseph, *Flying With the Eagle, Racing the Great Bear*. BridgeWater Books, 1993. (8–12)
Bruchac has collected coming of age stories from sixteen Native American tribes, each demonstrating a value held sacred by that tribe. This is a great resource when studying adolescence in various cultures.

Applications: Values:
Language Arts–Dramatization,   Courage, Self–
  Creative writing   reliance, Honor
Social Studies–Comparison of
  values with one's own culture

Buck, Pearl S. (compiler), *Fairy Tales of the Orient*. Simon and Schuster, 1965. (5–12)
Having spent much of her life in the Orient, Pearl Buck is certainly qualified to select the best stories from a variety of cultures. Through a brief preface to each tale, she helps the reader to understand a bit more about the ethnic group represented.

Applications: Values:
Language Arts–Storytelling,   Morals of ethnic
  Research common motifs   groups, Courage
Social Studies–Units on specific   Right prevails over
  countries   wrong

Carle, Eric, *Eric Carle's Treasury of Classic Stories for Children.* **Orchard books, 1988. (K–8)**
Carle has chosen twenty-two well-known stories by Hans Christian Andersen, the Brothers Grimm, and Aesop to present in this collection. The oversize volume is brightened by Carle's familiar collage illustrations and contains brief biographical sketches of the contributors.

Applications:
Language Arts–Reading aloud,
   Storytelling, Dramatization

Values:
Humor, Courage,
Family Unity, Wisdom

Chaucer, Geoffrey, *Chanticleer and the Fox.* **Retold and illus. by Barbara Cooney. Thomas Crowell Co., 1948. (K–3, 8–12)**
This is an adaptation of the "Nun's Priest's Tale" from *The Canterbury Tales.* The proud rooster is tricked by the fox but learns his lesson in time to outwit his pursuer.

Applications:
Language Arts–Write another
   conclusion. Dramatization
Social Studies–Middle Ages

Values:
Humility, Creative
thinking

Chase, Richard (compiler), *The Grandfather Tales.* **Illus. by Berkeley Williams, Jr., E. M. Hall and Co., 1948. (5–8)**
Richard Chase personally collected the folk tales in this classic volume from original sources in North Carolina, Virginia and Kentucky. The reader may recognize "The Outlaw Boy" as the more familiar "Robin Hood" or "Catskins" and "Ashpet" as "Cinderella." The mountain versions of the better-known stories reveal the values and sense of humor of the rural setting from which they came.

Applications:
Language Arts–Dramatization,
Compare with similar versions
   of individual stories
Social Studies–Appalachia

Values:
Humor, Courage,
Independence,
Resourcefulness

Chase, Richard (compiler), *The Jack Tales.* **Houghton Mifflin, 1943. (5–12)**
Ageless stories of the hero "Jack," who outwits giants, royalty, and just plain neighbors, fill this collection of Southern mountain stories collected by Richard Chase. Valuing the humor and wisdom of the Appalachian culture, this folklorist traveled through the hills and recorded, in authentic tone and style, these memorable tales.

Applications:
Language Arts–Storytelling,
   Dramatization
Social Studies–Appalachia

Values:
Humor, Creativity,
Respect for the culture

Climo, Shirley, *The Egyptian Cinderella.* **Illustrated by Ruth Heller. Harper Trophy, 1989. (K–8)**
According to the author's note, this is one of the world's oldest Cinderella stories, originally recorded in the first century B.C. Having some of the same elements as the familiar French version, this story has the unique quality of containing both fact and fable. Authentic in artistic detail and mood, it is a beautiful book and an elegant addition to the Cinderella collection.

Applications:
Social Studies–Egypt
Psychology–Orphans, Prejudice

Values:
Creativity,
Coping with adversity

Climo, Shirley, *The Korean Cinderella.* **Illustrated by Ruth Heller. HarperCollins, 1993. (K–8)**
Climo and Heller have created an elegant combination of textual and visual beauty in this oriental version of a familiar story. Korean culture is authentically portrayed in both the brightly colored artwork and the story of how obedience in the face of adversity is rewarded.

Applications:
Language Arts–Compare to
   Cinderella stories
Social Studies–Korea
Art–Study Oriental works

Values:
Obedience, Kindness,
Perseverance,
Respect for nature

DeLeeuw, Adele, *Legends: Folk Tales of Holland.* **Thomas Nelson & Sons, 1965. (5–12)**
A delightful cross-section of more than twenty-five folktales of the Netherlands fill this work. Stories range in theme from dragons in the cellar to a shepherd who outwits Charles V and saves his beloved abbot.

Applications:
Language Arts–Storytelling,
  Dramatization
Social Studies–Holland

Values:
Loyalty, Honor,
Virtue, Love,
Courage

dePaola, Tomie (adapter and illustrator) *The Legend of the Bluebonnet: An Old Tale of Texas.* **G.P. Putnam's Sons, 1983. (4–8)**
The Comanche people have been without rain for a long time and are desperate for its healing showers. When the Shaman reports that the sacrifice of something valuable will bring blessing from the gods, a lonely little girl responds in a totally selfless way. A memorable story with starkly beautiful illustrations.

Applications:
Art–Create flower collage
Social Studies–Texas, Indians of
  North America

Values
Sacrifice, Faith

dePaola, Tomie (adapter), *The Legend of Old Befana: An Italian Christmas Story.* **Harcourt Brace Jovanovich, 1980. (K–4)**
Old Befana is always working and never has time for visiting. One day a procession of wealthy men come by her house and ask the way to Bethlehem. They are looking for the Child King. She is too busy to pay much attention, but later reconsiders when it is too late.

Applications:
Language Arts–Create own
  Christmas story
Social Studies–Italy

Values:
Taking time for others,
Gift giving

Edmonds, I. G. (compiler), *Trickster Tales.* **J. B. Lippincott, 1966. (K–12)**
Whether he is called Tyl Eulenspiegel (Germany), Ooka (Japan), Don Coyote (Mexico), or a host of other names, the trickster exists in folktales world-wide. Edmonds has brought together eighteen stories that demonstrate the antics of the sly one, whatever his country of origin.

Applications: Values:
Language Arts–Reading aloud,   Humor
  Dramatization
Social Studies–Country units

Finlay, Winifred, *Tattercoats and Other Folktales.* **Illustrated by Shirley Hughes. Harvey House, 1976. (5–8)**
This collection of folktales comes from the British Isles. Some of the more tellable tales are "The Old Handmill," a story of how the sea became salty; "Wee Robin Redbreast," a story which highlights the wisdom of nature's creatures; and "Tattercoats," the British version of Cinderella.

Applications: Values:
Language Arts–Storytelling,   Creativity, Wisdom,
  Reading aloud   Cultural awareness
Social Studies–England, Scotland,
  Ireland

Gilman, Phoebe (adapter and illustrator), *Something from Nothing.* **Scholastic, 1992. (K–4)**
A grandparent's devotion and ingenuity are the threads that weave together this Jewish folktale. As young Joseph matures, the treasured blanket from his infancy is transformed into other useful items by his grandfather, who is a tailor. Engaging illustrations reveal an intimate view of Jewish life in this lovely oversized book.

Applications: Values:
Language Arts–Reading aloud,   Love, Creativity,
  Dramatization, Storytelling   Family Unity
Social Studies–Jewish life

Hague, Michael (compiler and illustrator), *Aesop's Fables.* **Holt, Rinehart & Winston, 1985.** (4–12)
Michael Hague's elegantly cozy illustrations add a greater dimension to the thirteen fables he has selected for this volume. Each story is made more memorable through this gifted artist's interpretation.

Applications:
Art–Appreciation of Hague's work
Language Arts–Compare to other
  Aesop versions, Storytelling

Values:
Humor, Wisdom

Hamilton, Virginia, *The People Could Fly: American Black Folktales.* **Illustrated by Leo and Diane Dillon. Alfred A. Knopf, 1985.** (K–12)
Hamilton has brought together stories from the African-American slave days. In her extensive introduction she explains the origin and organization of this collection. It is an important contribution to the history of an oppressed people and demonstrates how they used imagination to survive.

Applications:
Language Arts–Storytelling,
  Reading aloud
Social Studies–African American
  awareness, Slavery

Values:
Imagination, Humor,
Courage, Survival

Han, Suzanne Crowder, *The Rabbit's Judgment.* **Illustrated by Yumei Heo. Henry Holt and Co., 1991.** (K–8)
This delightful picture book is presented in two languages, Korean and English. A retelling of a Korean folktale, the story depicts the wisdom of Rabbit, who is often the hero of this country's traditional literature.

Applications:
Art–Korean art
Language Arts–Dramatization
Social Studies–Korea

Values:
Knowledge,
Wisdom in asking
advice

Harris, Joel Chandler (adapted by Van Dyke Parks), *Jump Again! More Adventures of Brer Rabbit.* **Illustrated by Barry Moser. Harcourt Brace Jovanovich, 1987.** (5–8)
Van Dyke Parks has simply made more readable the delightful stories first told by Joel Chandler Harris in the late 1800s, while retaining colloquial expressions, the personalities of the characters, and the flavor of the original tales. Brer Rabbit and his friends are a treat no generation should miss.

Applications: Values:
Language Arts–Reading aloud,   Humor, Ingenuity,
   Storytelling   Weak triumphs over
                                        strong

Hayes, Joe (compiler and adapter), *The Day It Snowed Tortillas.* **Illustrated by Lucy Jelinek. Mariposa Publishing, 1986.** (K–12)
These ten tales were collected from Spanish New Mexico by Joe Hayes, a former high-school English teacher turned storyteller. Reprinted three times in four years, this little volume contains stories the novice storyteller will enjoy sharing.

Applications: Values:
Language Arts–Reading aloud   Humor, Ingenuity,
Social Studies–New Mexico   Heritage

Hearn, Michael (compiler), *The Victorian Fairy Tale Book.* **Pantheon, 1988.** (5–12)
If there were one period in history that characterized the Golden Age of fairy tales, it would probably be the Victorian era. Hearn has compiled some of the best of the best in this volume. Browning, Dickens, McDonald, and Grahame are just a few contributors.

Applications: Values:
Language Arts–Reading aloud,   Courage, Loyalty,
   Storytelling   Good triumphs over
Social Studies–Victorian era   evil, Perseverance,
                                        Sacrifice, Honor

Hodges, Margaret (adapter), *Saint George and the Dragon.* **Illustrated by Trina Schart Hyman. Little Brown, 1984.** (K–8) Caldecott Award
This memorable little volume is a retelling of Edmund Spenser's *Faerie Queene.* The story contains all the elements essential to fantasy: a brave young man, a beautiful lady, a dragon, and the promise of the princess's hand, with the accompanying fame and fortune. Hyman's award winning illustrations are as fascinating as the text.

Applications: Values:
Art–Realism, Detail, Mood   Courage, Loyalty
Language Arts–Reading aloud
Social Studies–Middle Ages

Hunt, Angela Elwell (adapter), *The Tale of Three Trees.* **Illustrated by Tim Jonke. Lion Publishing.** (K–9)
In this traditional folktale, three trees have plans and dreams for their future. What actually happens to each is at first a disappointment, but the final result is much greater than they could have imagined. Soft illustrations enhance this thought-provoking tale.

Applications: Values:
Language Arts–Reading aloud,   Sacrifice, Patience,
  Dramatization   Humility

Jarrell, Randall (Translator), *Snow White and the Seven Dwarfs.* **Illustrated by Nancy Ekholm Burkert. Farrar, Strauss and Giroux, 1972.** (4–8) Caldecott Honor Book
In this retelling of the Grimms' tale of envy, deception, and the final triumph of love and goodness, Randall Jarrell has selected vivid, yet understated language for his translation. Burkert's award-winning illustrations go beyond the decorative to include interesting symbolism, as well as regal design and color.

Applications: Values:
Language Arts–Folktales,   Loyalty, Service
  Symbolism, Reading aloud
Social Studies–Germany

Kellogg, Steven (adapter and illustrator), *Chicken Little.*
William Morrow, 1985. (K–4)
Updated dialogue and inventive illustrations make this retelling of the
old story hilarious. The reader, privy to plans of that conniving Foxy
Loxy throughout (as he plans his menu), will smile at every rereading
as the villain gets his due.

Applications: Values:
Language Arts–Dramatization,   Courage, Humor
  Reading aloud, Storytelling
Art–Illustrated with captions

Kellogg, Steven (adapter and illustrator), *Johnny Ap-*
pleseed: A Tall Tale. **Morrow Junior Books, 1988. (K–4)**
This delightful book, full to the brim with rollicking illustration, is
just what the title suggests: a retelling of the Johnny Appleseed
legend. Kellogg begins with John Chapman's birth and concludes
with the acknowledgment that yet today there are those who claim to
have seen this famous planter of apple trees. The author sprinkles
text with hum and shares a history and geography lesson through
maps on the end pages.

Applications: Values:
Language Arts–Heroes, Tall tales,   Unselfishness,
Storytelling   Courage,
Social Studies–Pioneer life   Self–reliance

Kellogg, Steven (adapter and illustrator), *Pecos Bill.*
William Morrow and Co., 1986. (K–4)
The boisterous adventures of this legendary hero are retold and
illustrated with humor and rich detail in this oversized picture book.
From his trek west as a small child to his joyous wedding, Bill
bounds through the pages in true folk hero style.

Applications: Values:
Language Arts–Reading aloud,   Humor, Imagination
  Further information on Bill
Social Studies–Frontier life

Kherdian, David (compiler), *Feathers and Tails: Animal Fables From Around the World.* **Illustrated by Nonny Hogrogian. Philomel Books, 1992. (5–8)**
Caldecott artist Nonny Hogrogian joins her husband, Newbery Honor Award winner David Kheridan, in sharing ever-fresh animal fables from around the world. Some illustrations are lovely enough to frame, and the text reflects the wit and wisdom from areas as varied as Armenia and Alaska.

Applications:
Language Arts–Reading aloud
Social Studies–Countries included

Values:
Wisdom, Humor,
Cooperation,
Kindness, Friendship

Knowles, Sir James (compiler), *King Arthur and His Knights.* **Illustrated by Louis Rhead. Crown Publishers, 1986. (8–12)**
Based on Sir Thomas Malory's *Le Morte d'Arthur*, this handsome volume moves from the courtship of Arthur's parents to his fatal wounding. Love, loyalty, chivalry, bravery, and betrayal unfold as authentic illustrations enhance the medieval tone.

Applications:
Language Arts–Literature
Social Studies–England, Middle
    Ages

Values:
Bravery, Loyalty,
Honesty,
Self–sacrifice

Lang, Andrew (compiler), *The Blue Fairy Book.* **Illustrated by Ben Kutcher. David McKay, 1964. (K–12)**
The first edition of this classic collection of folk and fairy tales was published in 1889, and its contribution is considered as valuable to the contemporary reader as to its original audience. For his first volume, Lang chose stories that are most familiar, such as "Cinderella," "Sleeping Beauty," and "Dick Wittington and His Cat." Other volumes in the series also bear color names.

Applications:
Language Arts–Reading aloud,
    Storytelling, Dramatization

Values:
Courage, Loyalty,
Love, Good over evil

Lobel, Anita, *The Straw Maid*. Greenwillow Books, 1983. (K–4)
This simply-written folktale should have special appeal to young children because the protagonist is a child who demonstrates wisdom, courage, and creativity in problem solving. In the end, she gains wealth that will meet her family's needs for a lifetime.

Applications: Values:
Language Arts–Reading aloud,   Courage, Ingenuity,
  Easy reading, Storytelling,   Perseverance
  Dramatization, Creative
  writing

Lobel, Arnold, *Fables*. Harper & Row, 1980. (K–8)
Arnold Lobel has created a modern-day collection of brief stories with morals that would please even Aesop. Animals serve as both heroes and villains in this brief volume. The very young may not decipher the lesson in each story, but that will not hinder their enjoyment of a good tale.

Applications: Values:
Language Arts–Storytelling,   Creativity, Humility,
  Reading aloud, Creative writing,   Integrity, Patience
  Reader's theatre

Low, Alice (compiler), *The Family Read-Aloud Holiday Treasury*. Illustrated by Marc Brown. Trumpet Club, 1991. (K–12)
Short stories, chapters from favorite books, and poetry form the contents of this varied collection of Christmas gifts for children and parents alike. Reading from this work may well become a Christmas tradition.

Applications: Values:
Language Arts–Reading aloud,   Giving, Love,
  Recreational reading, Storytelling   Security, Faith
Art–Create a mural or mobile of
  favorite story or poem.

MacDonald, George, *The Christmas Stories of George MacDonald.* **Illustrated by Linda Hall Griffith. David C. Cook, 1981.** (4–8)
This collection of eight Christmas stories and poems by the master storyteller from Scotland is lavishly illustrated in Victorian style and will add much to traditional Christmas celebrations whether at home or at school. Stories range from castle to cottage, from town to country.

Applications:	Values:
Language Arts–Reading aloud,	Love, Giving,
Storytelling	Family Unity
Social Studies–Holidays,	

McKissack, Patricia and Frederick, *The Little Red Hen.* **Children's Press, 1985.** (K–3)
This is a retelling of the classic story of taking responsibility and gaining rewards. The McKissacks have used an easy-reading format and included a glossary of words basic to the vocabulary of beginning readers so that they may try sight-reading unfamiliar words before tackling the text. Dennis Hockerman's illustrations add much to this time-honored tale.

Applications:	Values:
Language Arts–Easy reading,	Cooperation,
Role playing, Reader's theatre	Responsibility

McKissack, Patricia and Frederick, *Cinderella.* **Illustrated by Tom Dunington, Children's Press, 1985.** (K–4)
To assist the begining reader, the McKissacks have included a glossary containing those words a novice reader should easily recognize. Simple sentences and attractive illustrations aid comprehension of this well-known fairy tale for the young reader.

Applications:	Values:
Language Arts–Easy reading (2–3),	Diligence, Love,
Remedial reading (3–4),	Pleasure
Prereading sequencing	

Moser, Barry (adapter and illustrator), *Tucker Pfeffercorn.* **Little, Brown & Co., 1994. (4–8)**
Barry Moser retells the story of Rumpelstiltskin with Southern country setting and dialogue. His illustrations of miners, the lovely Bessie Grace, and the hideous Tucker Pfeffercorn are so realistic that they could have been lifted from an old photograph album.

Applications:
Language Arts–Reading aloud, Storytelling, Comparison with other versions of Rumpelstiltskin

Values:
Courage, Love, Determination

O'Brien, Anne Sibley (adapter and illustrator), *The Princess and the Beggar: A Korean Folktale.* **Scholastic, 1993. (5–12)**
This single story volume reveals many of the cultural values that demonstrate the importance of folktales. Loyalty, wisdom, beauty, and humility are portrayed in a memorable story of princess-meets-peasant.

Applications:
Language Arts–Comparison with similar stories in other cultures
Social Studies – Korea
Psychology–Respecting individuality

Values:
Individuality, Love, Wisdom, Loyalty, Danger of judging by appearances

Paterson, Katherine, *The King's Equal.* **Illustrated by Vladimir Vagin. Trumpet Book Club, 1992. (4–12)**
East and West collaborate in this folktale of wisdom, magic, and romance, as Paterson tells the story of a king who values the leadership of his future daughter-in-law just as highly as that of his son. Elaborate illustrations by the Russian artist Vladimir Vagin lend a special dignity to the work.

Applications:
Language Arts–Reading aloud, Recreational reading, Dramatization

Values:
Wisdom, Patience, Perseverance, Humility

Pyle, Howard (compiler and illustrator), *The Merry Adventures of Robin Hood.* **Penguin Books, 1985.** (9–12)
Pyle states that the purpose of his collection of Robin Hood stories is to share a bit of fun and good humor. The language of romance, fast-paced action, and satisfactory dispatch of villains create the delightful mix that has made this book a classic since its release in 1883.

Applications:
Language Arts–Legends,
Social Studies–E ngland, Middle
  Ages

Values:
Loyalty, Courage,
Concern for others

Schwartz, Alvin (collector), *Whoppers: Tall Tales and Other Lies.* **Illustrated by Glen Rounds. Lippincott, 1975.** (4–12)
Here is a book just loaded with lies that it's okay to tell. Whether they are called "windies" or "whoppers" or "gallyfloppers" they are all creative and humorous. The child who has been successful at little else will find victory in retelling these stories as there is no right or wrong–as long as it is exaggerated.

Applications:
Language Arts–Storytelling,
  Creative writing (write your
  own tall tale), Dramatization

Values:
Imagination, Humor,
Variety, Creativity,
Building self-esteem

Schoolcraft, Henry Rowe, edited by John Bierhorst, *The Fire Plume: Legends of American Indians.* **Illustrated by Alan E. Coher. Dial Press, 1969.** (All ages)
This is a collection of stories from the larger Algonquin tribes of the northeastern United States and Canada. The stories reveal cultural names and spiritual beliefs of the Chipppewa, Shawnee, Ottawa, and Monimee tribes. The format is appropriate for the beginning storyteller.

Applications:
Language Arts–Storytelling
Social Studies–Indian culture
Science–Weather

Values:
Cultural awareness,
Courage, Loyalty

Serraillier, Ian, *Beowulf the Warrior*. Oxford University Press, 1954. (8–12)
Retold in today's language, the epic poem loses none of its meaning or dignity in this version. Focusing on courage and leadership, this story holds as much value for young people as when first recorded 1000 years ago. Youth still must slay monsters in their own lives.

Applications: Values:
Literature–Epic poetry   Courage, Leadership

Shepard, Esther, *Paul Bunyan*. Harcourt, Brace & World, 1952. (4–12)
The legendary Paul Bunyan has been immortalized since the early 1860s. Part of the timelessness of his popularity is the result of his determination to tackle any task–often with humor and ingenuity. Although a logger by trade, his spirit is a reflection of basic American philosophy. Shepard has collected a representative sample of Bunyan's mighty antics that should provide both inspiration and amusement for readers or listeners.

Applications: Values:
Language Arts–Legends, Creative   Motivation, Humor,
  writing, Storytelling   Ingenuity
Social Studies–the Northwest

Smith, Philip (editor), *Japanese Fairy Tales*. Illustrated by Kokuzo Fujiyama. Dover Publications, 1992. (4–8)
In five brief stories the reader or listener is introduced to values stressed in Japanese culture. Respect for elders, obedience to parents, reverence for those in authority, and the binding force of giving one's word are stressed in this unabridged little book. It is enlightening to those who wish to know more about that ancient land, and makes an enriching addition to any library.

Applications: Values:
Language Arts–Reading aloud,   Respect, Obedience,
  Storytelling   Reliability, Cultural
Social Studies–Japan   awareness

Steptoe, John (adapter and illustrator), *Mufaro's Beautiful Daughters.* **Lothrop, Lee & Shepard, 1987. (K–12) Caldecott Honor Award**
This is a retelling of an African folktale with the Cinderella motif. The evil sister, rude and disrespectful, learns a lesson in kindness and humility as virtue is rewarded and she becomes the good sister's servant. Steptoe's rich illustrations add elegance to the story.

Applications: Values:
Language Arts–Compare to other   Kindness, Respect
  Cinderella stories, Dramatization

Van Allsburg, Chris, *The Wretched Stone.* **Houghton Mifflin, 1991. (4–12)**
This modern day fable is a tongue-in-cheek tale of sailors who are bewitched by a strange glowing stone that literally makes monkeys out of them. However, those who read are the first to recover, and that is just one subliminal message in this beautifully illustrated volume.

Applications: Values:
Language Arts–Reading aloud,   Analysis, Inference,
  Symbolism, Recreational reading   Humor

Yep, Laurence, *The Rainbow People.* **Harper & Row, 1989. (4–9)**
Yep retells stories that are the essence of a people transplanted in foreign soil. Leaving conditions that were intolerable and coming to conditions that sometimes were little better than endurable, the Chinese immigrants and subsequent generations have kept alive the spirit of their culture through the exchange of stories such as these.

Applications: Values:
Language Arts–Storytelling,   Cultural awareness,
Social Studies–China, America at   Heritage
  the turn of the century, Compare
  with similar stories from other
  ethnic groups

Young, Ed, *Lon Po Po: A Red-Riding Hood Story from China.* **Philomel Books, 1989.** (5–9) **Caldecott Medal**
Written lovingly, in almost poetic language, this story tells of the wickedness of an invading wolf, confronted by the bravery of three little Chinese girls, providing a suspenseful and beautifully illustrated version of an ancient tale. The mother has gone to visit grandmother and left her daughters with the admonition not to let anyone into their house. The deceiving wolf does not reckon with the cleverness of the girls.

Applications: Values:
Language Arts–Comparison with   Courage, Ingenuity,
   other stories of same motif   Obedience
Social Studies–China

Zemach, Harve (adapter), *Nail Soup: A Swedish Folktale.* **Illustrated by Margot Zemach. Follett, 1964.** (K–4)
The theme of this story is expressed by a homeless vagabond when he tells a stingy old lady that human beings are supposed to help each other. Through the cunning of the tramp and the cooperation of the old woman, both are gladdened and filled with food and friendship.

Applications: Values:
Language Arts–Compare with   Sharing, Creativity,
   other versions of story (*Stone*   Joy of Cooking
   Soup, Fiddler), Dramatization
Health–Make soup

Zemach, Harve (adapter), *Salt.* **Follett, 1965.** (K–4)
That which appears foolish to some may be wisdom in disguise. Such is the theme of this Russian folktale. Sibling rivalry, the value of common things, and a benevolent father are all aspects of this story that will make it a favorite with children and parents alike.

Applications: Values:
Language Arts–Reading aloud   Individuality, Courage,
Social Studies–Russia   Forgiveness
Health–Uses of salt

CHAPTER THREE

MODERN FANTASY

If Thomas Edison had not dreamed of things that seemed impossible, you might be reading this book by lamplight–or if Gutenberg had not invented the printing press, the existence of books published for masses of people would be only a dream. The point is that dreams or fantasies or belief in the impossible furnishes fertile ground for creation, discovery, and invention. All children have imagination. They will imagine *something*. It is our responsiblity as caring adults to feed that creative source healthy, stimulating food. Children who have a healthy fantasy life have a clearer idea of good and evil, of courage and cowardice, of kindness and injustice, than those surrounded only by the narrow world they can experience with their senses.

Modern fantasy dates back to 1865 and the publication of *Alice in Wonderland* by Lewis Carroll. Since that time, there has been a continual parade of authors and books that call on the reader to believe the unbelievable–as fantasy has been defined. There have sprung up distinct divisions in fantasy writing such as high or complex fantasy and, in contrast, common or light fantasy. Within those divisions are yet other subcategories, such as animal (*The Wind in the Willows*), adventure (*Peter Pan*), supernatural (*Tuck Everlasting*), science fiction (*A Wrinkle in Time*), and stories involving movement in time both forward (*The Giver*) and backward (*Building Blocks*), In this introduction, we will define only the broad categories of common and high fantasy, although all of the subcategories mentioned above are included in our selections.

Common fantasy simply asks the reader to believe in what the rational mind says is impossible. We might call it pretending written down. It appeals to the child's desire to have stuffed animals or real animals talk, to be able to fly, to go places and do things that a child would never be able to do. One timeless example of this type of book is *Winnie-the-Pooh* by A. A. Milne. This little volume appeals to children and adults because it is not only a good story, but also provides a wonderful escape from the "success" philosophy that drives modern society. Pooh and his friends in the Hundred Acre Wood are content to just be themselves, and if adventure should find them, they share it together. When it gets too dangerous, they call on the wisdom of Christopher Robin (aged about six) to resolve the problems.

Another example of light fantasy is E. B. White's masterpiece, *Charlotte's Web*. This unassuming little volume is such a great example of achievement that it appears as a standard in most children's literature textbooks. Children do not care about adult judgments, however; they love it just because it is a memorable story. Rich in teaching and learning potential, it is as popular with college students studying children's books as with the young ones themselves.

Marching in the parade of complex fantasy are those books that deal with lofty purposes, high ideals, and dangerous quests. Often the hero must endure hardship, risk his or her life or those of willing followers, as well as sacrifice something precious. They must also exhibit great courage and demonstrate selflessness. Leading this parade, perhaps, would be *The Chronicles of Narnia* by C. S. Lewis. Although this series may be seen as allegorical, it is also great adventure. First published in the 1950s, these books, represented in this collection by *The Lion, The Witch, and The Wardrobe,* have remained popular through numerous printings.

We believe that our selections include a balance between stories that cause the reader to ponder the deep meanings of life, and those that provide healthy escape from the same. Age, interest, and gender were considered in our choices and it was our goal to meet the needs of a broad spectrum of readers. We are recommending those works that reflect the spirit of this book and that we have seen to be loved by children and young adults.

Adams, Richard, *Watership Down*. Avon, 1972. (9–12)
Although Adams successfully transports his audience to the British countryside to experience life with a small group of displaced rabbits, the theme is unmistakably political. The reader is gripped by the plight of the rabbits as they struggle to find a new home in which democracy can thrive.

Applications:
Literature–Individual reading
  and group discussion
Government–Democracy vs.
  tyranny

Values:
Freedom, Unity,
Courage, Self-
sacrifice

Atwater, Richard and Florence, *Mr. Popper's Penguins*. Illustrated by Robert Lawson. Little Brown & Co., 1938. (1–4)
Twelve penguins arrive at the home of a humble impractical house painter and catapult him to fame through many hilarious adventures. A memorable story, enlivened by Caldecott-winning illustrator Robert Lawson, makes this a must for any library shelf. Fifty-three printings stand as a testimony to its timelessness.

Applications:
Language Arts–Reading aloud,
  Dramatization,
Science–Research penguins,
  Arctic life

Values:
Individuality, Humor,
Perseverance

Babbitt, Natalie, *Tuck Everlasting*. Farrar, Straus & Giroux, 1975. (4–6)
Having drunk inadvertently from a spring that halts aging and death, the Tuck family seems to be in an enviable situation. However, disclosure of their secret by an innocent little girl or a villainous stranger would result in certain tragedy.

Applications:
Language Arts–Symbolism,
  Creative writing
Psychology–Decision making

Values:
Loyalty, Honesty,
Family unity, Maturity,
Consequences of greed

Barrie, James M. *Peter Pan.* **Charles Scribner's Sons, 1950. (5–8)**
To read the original version of this classic is to enjoy the old story on a much higher level. Humor lights up the fact of having to grow up like a candle in the darkness of the unknown and uncertain world of adulthood. Barrie demonstrates an uncanny ability to write from a child's perspective.

Applications:
Language Arts–Reading aloud,
  Recreational reading
Psychology–Facing maturity

Values:
Taking responsibility,
Adventure, Loyalty,
Humor

Banks, Lynne Reid, *The Indian in the Cupboard.* **ABCClio, 1988. (4–8)**
What might happen if toys really did come to life? Omri, a little English boy, discovers both the thrill of owning a pocket-sized Indian and the responsibility of caring for another human life in this thought-provoking fantasy.

Applications:
Language Arts–Reading aloud,
  Recreational reading
Psychology–The sanctity of life
Social Studies–British life

Values:
Responsibility, Respect,
Kindness, Self-sacrifice

Baum, Frank L., *The Wonderful Wizard of Oz.* **Justin Knowles Publishing Group, 1900, 1987. (K–4)**
This landmark story of fantasy provides not only the foundation for many later fantasy stories, but encourages the character qualities of loyalty, courage, and cooperation. Since Dorothy and Toto are well known from the movie version of this story, it would benefit children to meet the original characters.

Applications:
Language Arts–Reading aloud,
  Dramatization
Art–Illustrate the story

Values:
Loyalty, Courage,
Cooperation

Bond, Michael, *A Bear Called Paddington*. Houghton Mifflin, 1958. (K–8)
First introduced to the Brown family at Paddington Station, London, but originally from Darkest Peru, this mischievous bear will capture the hearts of readers. Paddington, named for the station in which he was discovered, has much to learn about British life. His humorous antics and misadventures will have the young reader/listener asking for others in the series.

Applications: Values:
Language Arts–Reading aloud,   Humor, Patience,
  Recreational reading   Compassion

Carroll, Lewis, *Alice's Adventures in Wonderland*. Illustrated by Arthur Rackham. Weathervane Books, a facsimile of the 1907 edition. (4–9)
Recognized as the Father of Modern Fantasy, Carroll presents the reader with a groundbreaking book of sheer imagination. Although many tales have followed in its wake, every child should have the opportunity of reading *Alice's Adventures*, if for no other reason than because it is often quoted in literature, politics, business, psychology, and other professional fields.

Applications: Values:
Language Arts–Reading aloud,   Imagination, Humor,
  Recreational reading   Logic

Davoll, Barbara, *Secret at Mossy Roots Mansion*. Illustrated by Dennis Hockerman. Moody Press, 1992.
Dusty and Musty Mole, along with other junior detective agents, explore an old mansion and catch a band of thieves while learning a lesson about prejudice in this volume of Molehole Mysteries. Short chapters make this a natural to read aloud. Imaginative illustrations decorate each page.

Applications: Values:
Language Arts–Reading aloud   Acceptance, Courage,
  Independent reading   Friendship

DuBois, William Pene, *The Twenty-One Balloons.* **Viking Press, 1947. (6–9)**
During the late 1800s, Professor William Waterman Sherman landed on the volcanic island of Krakatoa only to find its inhabitants were inventors of amazing mechanical wonders. This selection contains absurd humor and crazy logic and could provide the basis for much class discussion.

Applications: Values:
Science–Inventions, Aviation   Inventiveness, Humor
History–Government

Grahame, Kenneth, *The Wind in the Willows.* **Kestrel Books, 1983. (5–12)**
First published in 1908, this tale of friendship, foibles, pride, and downfall has delighted readers and listeners for generations. Toad of Toad Hall and his friends will cause the reader to laugh at their antics and to weep at the beauty of Grahame's prose. This book is a memorable choice for reading aloud in family times.

Applications: Values:
Language Arts–Reading aloud,   Friendship, Humor,
  Vocabulary, Recreational   Loyalty
  Reading

Jacques, Brian, *Mossflower.* **Illustrated by Gary Chalk, Philomel, 1988. (5–8)**
This first book in its series is unique even in the fantasy genre. One does not usually think of a cat and mouse story as being of epic quality, but Jacques has managed to achieve that status. The greedy cat Tsarmina underestimates the courage of Martin the mouse and his cohorts as they attempt to throw off her cruel domination.

Applications: Values:
Language Arts–Gifted readers,   Courage, Loyalty,
  Compare with other epic   Self-sacrifice,
  fantasies   Ingenuity
Science–Research animals

Juster, Norton, *The Phantom Tollbooth.* **Knopf, 1989. (5–12)**

Readers who enjoy word play will find food for the verbal appetite in this story. Bored and thinking he has nothing to do, Milo finds himself transported to the lands of Dictionopolis (the city of letters) and Digitopolis (the city of numbers). His adventures guarantee that as long as he has letters and numbers, he will never again be bothered by boredom.

Applications: Values:
Language Arts–Recreational   Creativity, Ingenuity
  reading, Develop a board game
Art–Create the cities
Mathematics–Counting, Time

Lawhead, Stephen R., *In the Hall of the Dragon King.* **Crossway, 1982. (9–12)**

Young Quentin, novice in the priesthood of the god Ariel, gives up his goals in life to seek out the One who embodies all good. His mission, to deliver a message to his newly chosen king, is filled with danger and adventure. This is the first of the Dragon King trilogy.

Applications: Values:
Language Arts–Compare to   Courage, Perseverance,
  The Hobbit and the Pendragon   Loyalty, Good over evil
  Cycle, Dramatization
Social Studies–England

Lawhead, Stephen R., *The Tale of Jeremy Vole.* **Lion, 1990. (K–4)**

When the Great Blue Heron appears suddenly to Jeremy to warn him of a coming flood, the little introverted animal is startled. When the large bird also tells Jeremy that it is his job to warn others, he is more than a little reluctant. His adventures make an exciting story.

Applications: Values:
Language Arts–Reading aloud,   Courage, Persistence,
  Recreational reading   Sacrifice
Science–Research river animals

Lawhead, Stephen R., *Taliesin.* **Crossway Books, 1987. (8–12)**
This first volume of the Pendragon Cycle chronicles the adventurous life of the Princess Charis, who, barely escaping with her life from the ill-fated Atlantis, finds a homeland as well as powerful love in the land of the Celts. Other volumes in the series include *Merlin* and *Arthur.*

Applications:
Literature–Compare with other
   Arthurian legends
History–British Isles

Values:
Courage, Loyalty

Lawson, Robert (author and illustrator), *Ben and Me.* **Little, Brown and Co., 1939. (5–8)**
Lawson refers to himself as the editor and illustrator of this little classic. According to the "author," Amos Mouse, he is the real brain behind Ben Franklin's inventions and diplomatic victories. The collaboration between man and mouse results in a work that is both historically and humorously successful.

Applications:
Language Arts–Reading aloud
Social Studies–Research Franklin,
   Unit on Revolutionary War, France

Values:
Friendship, Ingenuity,
Faithfulness, Humor

Lawson, Robert (author and illustrator), *Mr. Revere and I.* **Little, Brown & Company, 1953. (5–8)**
Children will delight in the view of history from Paul Revere's horse, Scheherazade. Delightful drawings enliven the adventurous story, depicting one of the first heroes of the Revolutionary War as a concerned husband and father and a person who is especially attentive to his faithful mount.

Applications:
Language Arts–Recreational
   reading, Reading aloud
History–Revolutionary War

Values:
Humor, Family life,
Courage, Loyalty

Lawson, Robert (author and illustrator), *Rabbit Hill.* **Viking Press, 1944. (K–4) Newbery Medal**
This beloved Newbery Medal winner gives the reader a rabbit's eye view of man, dogs, life, winter, and other animals. Little Georgie, Uncle Analdas, and other creatures are so realistic that they will be remembered as almost human long after the book is completed.

Applications:
Language Arts–Recreational
reading, Reading aloud
Science–Animals, Ecology,
Seasons

Values:
Kindness, Security,
Humor

L'Engle, Madeleine, *A Wrinkle in Time.* **Farrar, Straus and Giroux, 1962. (5–12)**
Instead of creating main characters that are beautiful and popular, L'Engle allows a rather Plain Jane with braces on her teeth and impossible hair to be her heroine. Her partner in adventure is a friend who feels that no one in his family really cares about him. Their mission is to save a life, a mind, and possibly a civilization.

Applications:
Language Arts–Reading aloud
Recreational reading
Science–Time/space relationships

Values:
Gifted child, Courage,
Self-acceptance,
Family unity

Lewis, C. S., *The Lion, The Witch and The Wardrobe.* **Illustrated by Pauline Baynes. Macmillan, 1950. (5–12)**
In this introduction to the series, The Chronicles of Narnia, the Pevensie children have been sent away from London because of air raids during World War II. In the home of an old college professor, they find a mysterious wardrobe that leads them to a magical land where they meet talking animals, including a powerful Lion, and find new resources within themselves.

Applications:
Language Arts–Reading aloud,
Symbolism, Dramatization

Values:
Courage, Unselfishness,
Team work, Integrity

Lofting, Hugh, *The Story of Dr. Dolittle.* **Lippincott, 1920, 1948. (K–8)**
A classic story of talking animals and a doctor with a great love for his pets, this is a book that should be available to all children. While the younger ones may enjoy hearing it read aloud, the older ones will enjoy tackling this first book in a series on animals, adventures, and imagination to read for themselves.

Applications:
Language Arts–Reading aloud,
   Recreational reading
Science–Care of pets

Values:
Imagination, Humor,
Thoughtfulness

Lowry, Lois, *The Giver.* **Houghton Mifflin, 1993. (9–12)**
Is the ideal world the one in which there is no conflict, poverty, unemployment, divorce, injustice, or inequality? Twelve-year-old Jonas receives his special assignment as Keeper of Memories in such a society. His choice is to help preserve his society the way it is, or to search for another. This provocative novel is written in a simple, understated prose leaving the reader with much to ponder.

Applications:
Language Arts–Reading aloud,
   Creative writing, Discussion
Government–Types of society

Values:
Sanctity of life,
Individuality, Courage
Creativity

Mains, David and Karen, *Tales of the Kingdom.* **Illustrated by Jack Stockman. David C. Cook, 1983. (4–12)**
Rich in symbolism, this collection of stories set in the realm of a nurturing Caretaker portrays both children and adults in crises. All are faced with decisions that will strengthen or weaken their character. Both adventure and nearly poetic prose provide the literary vehicles for each episode.

Applications:
Language Art–Reading aloud,
   Recreational reading,
   Dramatization

Values:
Decision making,
Courage, Friendship,
Self-acceptance

McKinley, Robin, *Beauty: A Retelling of Beauty and the Beast.* **Harper & Row, 1978. (5–12)**

McKinley has taken this somewhat enigmatic folktale and created a family and protagonist so realistic that they could be the reader's next-door neighbors. Such realism makes the sacrifice that is required of Beauty so much more terrible to consider. This would make a great read-aloud book even for middle schoolers.

Applications:	Values:
Language Arts–Reading aloud, Individual reading, Introduction to fairy tales	Family unity, Courage, Surviving adversity, Sacrifice, Loyalty, Love

Milne, A. A., *Winnie–the–Pooh.* **Illustrated by Ernest H. Shepard. E. P. Dutton, 1926, 1976. (K–4)**

Edward Bear, better known by his friends as Winnie-the-Pooh, may be a bear with little brain, but that does not prevent his adventures and misadventures in the Hundred Acre Wood. Though our hero is a stuffed animal, his friends include real residents of the Wood as well as his mentor, six-year-old Christopher Robin. This book is one of a series based on the lively yet tender exploration and expeditions of perhaps the most beloved bear in British history.

Applications:	Values:
Language Arts–Recreational reading, Dramatization	Friendship, Cooperation, Trust, Humility, Humor

Nesbit, Edith, *The Book of Dragons.* **Dell Yearling Books, 1900, 1990, (5–8)**

Edith Nesbit has compiled some original and humorous ideas about dragons in this little book. For every dragon lover, there is a story to tickle the fancy. I think my favorite is "The Dragon Tamers," which ends with the moral that one should be sure to feed the cat, or it may turn into a dragon.

Applications:	Values:
Language Arts–Storytelling, Creative writing Art–Collage	Humor, Friendship, Contentment, Courage Responsibility

Norton, Mary, *The Borrowers*. Illustrated by Beth and Joe Krush. Harcourt, Brace & World, 1952. (K–8)
This is the first in a series of stories about tiny people who take up residence in homes that are quiet and quite structured. Following a strict schedule is a must so that the Borrowers will know when it is safe to "borrow" items needed for their survival.

Applications:
Language Arts–Reading aloud,
  Puppetry, Creative writing
Art–Shadow boxes

Values:
Creativity, Courage,
Family unity

O'Brien, Robert, *Mrs. Frisby and the Rats of NIMH*. Atheneum, 1971. (5–12) Newbery Award
Imaginative and compelling throughout, this work leaves the reader in suspense even as it concludes. A unique animal story, it provides fuel for discussion among future scientists. The prevailing tenet is that kindness may exist on any level of life, and that luxury spoils those whose way of life is made too easy.

Applications:
Psychology–Social relationships
Social Studies–Comparing
  governments
Science–Implication of animal
  experimentation

Values:
Analysis, Courage,
Cooperation

Sharp, Margery, *The Rescuers: A Fantasy*. Illustrated by Garth Williams. Little, Brown & Co., 1959. (K–8)
Adventure, courage, daring, and romance all await the lover of mouse tales in this delightful story. The smallest creatures survive and triumph as they attempt to rescue a poet who has been incarcerated in the Black Castle.

Applications:
Language Arts–Reading aloud,
  Recreational reading

Values:
Courage, Friendship,
Humor

Silverstein, Shel (author and illustrator), *The Giving Tree.* **Harper & Row, 1964. (K–12)**
This simple story of love and growing to maturity has an appeal for all ages. A nameless little boy is loved by a tree, and loves her back as only a child can. As time passes, the boy grows older and the tree grows to maturity. In the relationship, the tree gives and the boy takes, yet in the end, both are happy as need brings mutual respect and appreciation.

Applications: Values:
Language Arts–Creative writing   Self-sacrifice, Maturity,
Science–Ecology   Creativity, Sharing

Tolkien, J. R. R., *The Hobbit.* **Houghton Mifflin, 1988. (9–12)**
Desiring only to remain in his comfortable hole in the ground, Bilbo Baggins, a hobbit, is called to lead a small group of dwarves on an adventure to reclaim treasure from a thieving dragon. High adventure, humor, and good triumphing over evil make this a memorable quest story. The saga is continued in the *Lord of the Rings Trilogy.* The story is also available for home viewing on video cassette.

Applications: Values:
Language Arts–Recreational   Courage, Humility,
   reading, Compare to film version   Cooperation, Friendship

Voigt, Cynthia, *Building Blocks.* **Fawcett Juniper, 1984. (5–8)**
This time travel story takes a young boy back to his father's childhood, opening doors to understanding his parents which were previously closed to him. Although there is some objectionable language, it is minimal and the empathy that takes place between father and son is significant, believable, and touching.

Applications: Values:
Psychology–Family understanding   Family unity, Respect,
Language Arts–Recreational   Tolerance
   Reading, Creative writing

White, E. B., *Charlotte's Web*. Illustrated by Garth Williams. Harper & Row, 1952. (4–8)
A story of sacrifice and friendship, of life and death, of cowardice and courage, this has become a classic of children's literature. The runt piglet and a spider who is both magical and wise team up to create a memorable story that is a must for every library shelf.

Applications:
Language Arts–Reading aloud,
  Recreational reading
Science–Research farms, pigs, and
  spiders

Values:
Sacrifice, Humor,
Friendship

White, E. B., *The Trumpet of the Swan*. Illustrated by Edward Franscino. Harper & Row, 1970. (5–8)
White has created a winning combination of animal-human relationships. Sam, the boy, helps Louis, the voiceless trumpeter swan, learn to read, write, and play the trumpet. Louis earns money to pay for damages done by his father in acquiring the instrument.

Applications:
Language Arts–Reading aloud,
  Recreational reading
Science–Swans
Health–Dealing with handicaps

Values:
Responsibility,
Compassion,
Perseverance

Williams, Margery, *The Velveteen Rabbit*. Illustrated by David Jorgesen. Random House, 1985. (K–4)
This touching story of what it means to be real and the discomfort of change has appeal across generations. First published in 1922, this fantasy of a toy rabbit remains as beloved today as it was more than half a century ago. Random House has equipped this version with an audio tape read by Meryl Streep.

Applications:
Language Arts–Reading aloud,
Psychology–Discuss being real
Art–Collage of stuffed animals

Values:
Friendship, Maturity,
Accepting change

Yep, Lawrence, *The Dragon of the Lost Sea.* **Harper & Row, 1982. (5–8)**
An unlikely ally in battle against a powerful witch is the skinny orphan boy, Thorn. Yet Shimmer, the dragon, discovers that she can trust him and must rely on him if she is to regain the lost sea of her ancestors. Excellent writing with unexpected twists that will hook the most reluctant reader.

Applications: Values:
Language Arts–Creative writing   Imagination, Humor,
    Reading aloud   Friendship, Courage,
                                       Perseverance

CHAPTER FOUR
MULTICULTURAL BOOKS

Much of children's view of themselves and their world comes from the books that they read. Images of real, positive characters living in situations similar to their own reinforce their confidence, saying "You are important." Conversely, lack of people like themselves or negative, stereotyped pictures say, "You do not matter." Supplying children with well-written literature from diverse cultural backgrounds informs them about themselves and helps them to have a truer picture of others. Some have predicted a ratio of one-third of school-age children in America coming from African-American, Asian-American, or Latino backgrounds by the year 2000. Providing books that reflect these various cultures and languages is becoming an increasingly important issue.

Of the types of books published for children that can fill this need for multicultural literature, perhaps the most familiar classification would be titles translated from other languages. Folk stories such as the Chinese *Tikki-Tikki-Tembo* (Mosel), the Russian *Peter and the Wolf* (Sergei Prokofiev), and the Native American *The Legend of the Bluebonnet* (Tomie DePaola) would fall into this category. Written in English, but picturing life in other countries, books such as *Crow Boy* by Taro Yashima, about a young mountain boy who is not immediately accepted by the other village school children, or Meindert DeJong's *Wheel on the School*, about Dutch children who work together to bring the storks back to their village, give a strong sense of the culture they represent while expressing emotions commonly felt by all children.

Within a country as culturally diverse as the United States, there is a richness of racial and ethnic traditions from which to draw. Ezra Jack Keats has been successful in drawing positive contemporary stories around African-American children living in a city setting. *Working Cotton* (Caldecott Honor, 1993) written by Sherley Ann Williams, weaves a warm family picture with hauntingly lovely illustrations about migrant farm workers in California. Authors such as Hadley Irwin (*Kim/Kimi*) and Linda Crew (*Children of the River*) have gone further in expressing the pressures of reconciling life in two cultures. Their heroines both struggle in coming to terms with their Asian descent while living the lives of modern American teenagers. A. E. Cannon has demonstrated how these cultural tensions affect relationships in his story of a Native American boy who was reared by a white family in *The Shadow Brothers*. Through the characters they read about, children are able to see positive ways of dealing with the situations which they themselves face.

For some, the stories offer understanding of the difficult situations in which others live. They provide a way to become aware of people from different races, to gain respect for their way of living, and hopefully to reduce prejudice by presenting positive information about other cultures. Whether these stories describe various cultures within the reader's own country or are international stories portraying the lives of people of other countries, they can help the reader understand that people of various cultures have the same fears, desires and dreams as their own, offsetting the crisis coverage of the news media which tends to focus on issues that divide.

Multicultural books encourage attitudes of acceptance and appreciation in children toward people who may be different from themselves. They build interest in the world beyond children's own everyday experience by helping to bring to life the history, traditions, and people that they see on television or read about in history books. Rather than break down national and ethnic pride, books like *The Sign of the Beaver* by Elizabeth George Speare, describing the friendship and mutual dependence between a white colonial boy and a Native American, can increase understanding. They can help people live together more peacefully with mutual respect and greater appreciation for their own nationality's unique contributions to society.

One way books can encourage understanding is to show the awful effects of prejudice and man's inhumanity to those different than himself. *Number the Stars* by Lois Lowry, *The Return* by Sonia Levitin, and *The Endless Steppe* by Esther Hautzig fill this role with haunting pictures of suffering countered by the indomitable strength of the human spirit in response to unreasoning persecution.

To promote true understanding, it is important that the written and illustrated details of the lifestyles portrayed be accurate from the point of view of someone living inside the cultural group represented. This must be done without exaggeration or romanticizing. Characters should be well-rounded and presented realistically rather than being used just to prove a point. Stereotyping must be vigorously avoided. As with any category of literature, multicultural books need to maintain a good story line, with authentic illustrations and a dialogue that maintains the integrity of the dialect without being difficult to read.

Armstrong, William, *Sounder.* **Harper & Row, 1969. (6–12) Newbery Award**
Armstrong graphically portrays the lifestyle that existed for many black families throughout the South in the early 1900s. The sights, sounds, hunger, fear, cruelty, and loyalty which existed are presented in a sensitive style.

Applications:
Language Arts–Creative writing,
    Dramatization, Compare to
    To Kill a Mockingbird
History–Race relations, African-
    Americans

Values:
Courage,
Perseverance

Avery, Susan, and Linda Skinner, *Extraordinary American Indians.* **Children's Press, 1992. (5–12)**
The authors present straightforward biographical information about the lives of over fifty Indian leaders who lived from the eighteenth century to the present. Also covered are major events in the history of Indian/Anglo-American relations.

Applications:
History–Indians of North America,
    Research one tribe or one famous
    individual, Cultural Awareness

Values:
Determination,
Courage

Bartone, Elisa, *Peppe The Lamplighter.* **Illustrated by Ted Lewin. Lothrop, Lee & Shepard, 1993. (K–4) Caldecott Honor Book**
The poetic prose of Elisa Bartone combined with the luminous illustrations of Ted Lewin creates a poignant story of the tenement streets of Little Italy in New York City at the turn of the century. Peppe will capture the heart of the reader as he takes a job as lamplighter to support his ailing father and seven sisters.

Applications:
History–Immigration,
Psychology–Cross-generational
    relations

Values:
Family loyalty, Work
ethic

Baylor, Byrd, *Amigo.* **Illustrated by Garth Williams. Aladdin, 1989.** (1–4)
Francesco wants a dog very much, but his family must work hard just to provide food for themselves. There are no scraps left over to feed a pet. Fortunately, while playing in the desert, Francesco finds a prairie dog who is looking for a boy to tame.

Applications:	Values:
Social Studies–Mexico	Friendship
Science–Animals, Desert, Pets	

Bemelmans, Ludwig (author and illustrator), *Madeline's Rescue.* **Viking Press, 1951.** (K–4)
Twelve little girls step out through the streets of Paris and into the reader's heart as the author spins a tale of humor and suspense. The smallest and most precocious of these children, Madeline, is saved from drowning by a dog whom the girls promptly decide to adopt. With rhyming text and engaging illustrations, the author draws children along on this unpredictable adventure.

Applications:	Values:
Social Studies–France	Humor, Friendship
Psychology–Orphans	

Bishop, Claire, *Twenty and Ten.* **Illustrated by William Pene du Bois. Viking Press, 1952.** (5–8)
During the German occupation of France in World War II, twenty boarding school children are asked to share their home and their food with ten young Jewish refugees, who are fleeing to Switzerland in an attempt to escape the Nazi holocaust. They must make a difficult choice whether to share their small food ration with ten more mouths. They also display real courage by remaining silent when Nazi soldiers come looking for the Jewish children.

Applications:	Values:
History–World War II, Jews,	Courage, Sacrifice,
Refugees	Ingenuity

Bunting, Eve, *How Many Days to America? A Thanksgiving Story.* **Illustrated by Beth Peck. Clarion, 1982. (K–4)**
To escape persecution in their country, families join in a perilous boat trip to America. After enduring storms, pirates, and lack of food, they arrive in America to a warm welcome on Thanksgiving Day.

Applications:	Values:
Social Studies–Immigration, Refugees, Trace one's roots	Courage, Hope, Determination
Language Arts–Creative writing (Describe what items you would take if you had to leave your home)	

Cannon, A. E., *The Shadow Brothers.* **Delacorte Press, 1990 (6–12)**
Henry Yazzi, reared by the Jenkins family as a brother to their son Marcus, never questions his Navajo background until he begins to approach manhood. As Henry struggles with issues of his identity, Marcus wrestles with jealousy and confusion over Henry's pulling away from their family. In the end, they both come to a greater understanding of themselves and their relationships.

Applications:	Values:
Language Arts–Journaling	Loyalty, Ethnic respect
Psychology–Foster parents, Biracial families	

Carlson, Natalie, *The Empty Schoolhouse.* **Harper & Row, 1965. (4–6) ALA Notable Book**
The desegregation of parochial schools in Louisiana brought happiness to Lullah, for now she could attend classes with her best friend Oralee Fleury. However, when the appearance of two strangers in town brings abusive phone calls and the threat of violence, Lullah must make a difficult decision.

Applications:	Values:
Social Studies–Race relations	Courage, Friendship,
Psychology–Decision making	

Cohen, Barbara, *Molly's Pilgrim*. Illustrated by Michael J. Deraney. Lothrop, Lee & Shepard, 1983. (K–4)
Molly, a recent arrival from Russia, is made fun of by the girls in her third grade class because of her old-country clothing. However, when Molly brings Mama's Pilgrim doll to school for a Thanksgiving project, her teacher helps the class realize that Molly and her family are modern-day pilgrims who have come to America for the same religious freedom the early Pilgrims sought.

Applications:
Social Studies–Immigration,
 Cultural awareness
Thanksgiving

Values:
Individuality, Heritage,
Family unity

Crew, Linda, *Children of the River*. Dell, 1989. (9–12)
Fleeing the Khmer Rouge army with her aunt's family, Sundara leaves her parents, brother, and sister in Cambodia when she is thirteen. Now living in America, she struggles to fit in at school while trying to please her traditional Cambodian aunt and uncle at home. If she adopts American ways, will she be disloyal to her family and the country she left behind?

Applications:
Social Studies–Immigration,
 Cambodia, Compare cultures
Psychology–Effects of war,
 Parent/child relations

Values:
Obedience,
Family loyalty

Cruz, Martel, *Yagua Days*. Illustrated by Jerry Pinkney. Dial Press, 1976. (K–4)
When Adam, who was born in New York city, hears the adults talking about "yagua days" every time it rains, he is curious. To him rainy days are boring. Then his parents take him to Puerto Rico to visit his uncle and he find that "yagua days" are wonderful.

Applications:
Social Studies–Puerto Rico,
 Cultural awareness

Values:
Family unity

deAngeli, Marguerite (author and illustrator), *Yonie Wondernose.* Doubleday, 1944. (K–4) Caldecott Honor
Yonie, a seven-year-old Pennsylvania Dutch boy, is called "Wondernose" because he wants to investigate everything he sees. When his parents go visiting overnight and he is left with his grandmother to care for the farm, he has a difficult time restraining his curiosity long enough to do all of the chores.

Applications: Values:
Social Studies–Rural life, Amish   Dependability, Curiosity

DeJong, Meindert, *The House of Sixty Fathers.* Illustrated by Maurice Sendak. Harper & Row, 1956. (6–12) Newbery Honor
Tien Pao is a winsome little Chinese boy who becomes separated from his family as the Japanese invade his country. He survives great hardship and suffering before finally being discovered by an American airman. When he is taken to the base, soldiers care for him until he is eventually reunited with his parents.

Applications: Values:
History–Chinese/Japanese relations   Courage, Responsibility,
  World War II   Endurance
Language Arts–Compare to *Year
  of Impossible Goodbyes*

DeJong, Meindert, *Wheel on the School.* Illustrated by Maurice Sendak. Harper Collins, 1954. (5–8) Newbery Medal
When Lina wonders why the storks no longer come to the village of Shora to roost, she arouses the interest of the children in attempting to bring them back. Facing many obstacles with strong determination, they soon involve the entire village in making their dream come true.

Applications: Values:
History–Holland   Determination,
Psychology–Physical handicaps   Ingenuity, Cooperation
Language Arts–Compare to *Hans
  Brinker and the Silver Skates*

Feelings, Muriel, *Jambo Means Hello: Swahili Alphabet Book.* **Illustrated by Tom Feelings. Dial Press, 1974. (K–4) Caldecott Honor**

Mrs. Feelings familiarizes children with traditional aspects of life in East Africa through her selection of twenty-four words chosen to illustrate each letter of the Swahili alphabet. Tom Feelings effectively illustrates the book with soft black and white, double–spread paintings.

Applications:
Language Arts–Alphabet
Social Studies–East Africa

Values:
Respect for another culture

Flack, Marjorie, *The Story about Ping.* **Illustrated by Kurt Wiese. Viking Press, 1933. (K–4)**

A young Chinese duck lives on a boat of the Yangtze River with his mother, father, sisters, brothers and other relatives. One evening when everyone is boarding the boat, Ping is late and is left behind. After several misadventures, he finds his way back to the safety of his owner and his family.

Applications:
Social Studies–China
Science–Ducks

Values:
Promptness, Obedience

Fox, Mem, *Koala Lou.* **Illustrated by Pamela Lofts. Harcourt Brace Jovanovich, 1988. (K–4)**

When new brothers and sisters are born into her family, Koala Lou thinks she has lost her mother's love. To win it back she feels she must win the gum tree climbing event in the Bush Olympics. When she does not win, but comes in second, she discovers that her mother's love was there all the time. Australian wildlife is skillfully presented throughout.

Applications:
Social Studies–Australia
Language Arts–Reading aloud
Psychology–Sibling rivalry

Values:
Determination, Family love

**Fox, Paula, *The Slave Dancer*. Illustrated by Eros Keith.
Bradbury Press, 1973.** (5–12) Newbery Medal
Jessie Bollier is kidnapped from the docks of New Orleans to play
his fife on a ship that carries captives from Africa to the slave
markets of Cuba. While on board, Jessie's music is used to make
the slaves dance to keep their muscles strong during the ocean
voyage. Shipwrecked by a storm, everyone is lost but Jessie and
one of the young captives.
Applications: Values:
History–Slavery   Cultural awareness

**Golenbock, Peter, *Teammates*. Illustrated by Paul Bacon.
Harcourt Brace, 1990.** (K–4)
As the first black player on any major league baseball team, Jackie
Robinson suffered much hostility and abuse from fans and opposing
players. In addition to his own talent and personal strength, the
friendship and support of fellow player Pee Wee Reese and owner
Branch Rickey helped Jackie to break down the walls of prejudice.
Applications: Values:
Social Studies–Race relations   Unselfishness, Courage,
Language Arts–African-Americans   Determination
  Biography
Sports–Baseball

**Hautzig, Esther, *The Endless Steppe: A Girl in Exile*.
Scholastic Press, 1970.** (9–12)
Torn from their home in North East Poland, the Rudomins are sent
to Siberia in 1941 as "capitalist" enemies of the state. There begins
a struggle for the food, clothing, and fuel needed to survive. The
Rudomins are not destroyed during this time of bitter hardship, but
emerge with new friends and deep affection and trust for one
another.
Applications: Values:
History–World War II, Russia,   Courage, Family love
  Jews
Psychology–Survival

Heide, Florence Parry, *The Day of Ahmed's Secret.* **Illustrated by Ted Lewin. Lothrop, Lee & Shepard, 1990. (K–4) Caldecott Honor**
Ahmed has a secret to share, but first, he must finish delivering bottles of fuel to his customers. As Ahmed wends his way through the streets, readers share with him the sights and sounds of modern Cairo. Although valuable for its many references to both ancient and modern aspects of Egyptian life, this title also conveys the universal joy of accomplishment and the importance of one's name.

Applications:	Values:
Social Studies–Egypt	Family unity,
Art–Colors	Responsibility, Cycle
Psychology–Importance of names	of life

Henderson, Lois T. *The Blessing Deer.* **David C. Cook, 1980. (9–12)**
Following the death of her mother, Ellen leaves Washington, D.C., to live with her relatives in Canada for one year. There she believes she will find an ideal society free of prejudice and hatred. As the year progresses, Ellen realizes that problems of the heart do not change with location.

Applications:	Values:
History–North American Indians	Forgiveness, Courage,
Psychology–Death of loved one	Acceptance

Hesse, Karen, *Letters from Rifka.* **Holt, 1992. (5–8)**
Twelve-year-old Rifka's journey from Russia to America is interrupted in Poland, where she contracts typhus, and in Belgium, where ringworm keeps her from boarding the boat with her family. Though her ringworm is healed, Rifka is held back again at Ellis Island until her hair begins to grow again. Through all of these difficulties, Rifka is sustained by the love of her Jewish family and her own strong spirit.

Applications:	Values:
History–World War II,	Family love and support,
Ellis Island, Immigration	Self-sacrifice

Hill, Elizabeth Starr, *Evan's Corner.* **Illustrated by Nancy Grossman. Holt, Rinehart and Winston, 1967. (K–4)**
Evan longs for a place of his own, but the family is too large and the apartment too small for him to have his own room. At mother's suggestion, he takes one corner and begins to fill it with special things all his own. When the corner is complete, Evan finds it strangely empty until his mother helps him see what is really missing.

Applications:
Psychology–Family, Sibling rivalry
Social Studies–City life

Values:
Cooperation, Sharing,
Giving

Hoffman, Mary, *Amazing Grace.* **Illustrated by Caroline Birch. Dial Books, 1991 (K–4) Caldecott Honor**
Grace, who loves acting out stories, volunteers to be Peter Pan in her class play. Encouraged by her mother and grandmother, Grace wins the part, rising above the comments of classmates who tell her she will not be chosen because she is a girl and she is black. Many full-page illustrations accent the story.

Applications:
Language Arts–Dramatization
Social Studies–Cultural awareness

Values:
Self-esteem, Determina-
tion

Irwin, Hadley, *Kim/Kimi.* **Puffin Books, 1987. (6–12)**
At sixteen, Kim Andres is secure in the love of her Irish-American mother, her younger half-brother, and her step-father. Yet, she feels incomplete within herself, because she knows that a part of her belongs to her deceased Japanese father, about whom she knows nothing. So she sets out alone to go across the country and find her father's family, knowing that she may be rejected, since they disowned him when he married out of his race.

Applications:
History–World War II
  Cultural Awareness
Psychology–Family
  heritage

Values:
Courage, Heritage,
Love, Loyalty

Keats, Ezra Jack (author and illustrator), *Peter's Chair.*
Harper and Row, 1967. (K–4)
When his parents paint his cradle, crib, and high chair pink for his
new baby sister, Peter is upset. He decides to take his dog Willie
along with his little chair and run away. As he sits down, however,
he finds that his chair is now too small for him and he decides that
maybe it will be all right for his baby sister to have his old things.

Applications: Values:
Psychology–Sibling rivalry   Sharing
Language Arts–Reading aloud

Leaf, Munro, *Wee Gillis.* **Illustrated by Robert Lawson.**
Viking Press, 1938. (K–4) Caldecott Honor
Wee Gillis is torn between choosing the life of a Lowlander, like his
mother's family, or a Highlander, like his father's. As he practices
the discipline to accomplish the tasks assigned to him by his
relatives on both sides of the family, he finds himself equipped to
make decisions regarding his own future.

Applications: Values:
Social Studies–Scotland   Discipline
Psychology–Self-concept, Family
  heritage

Lee, Harper, *To Kill a Mockingbird.* **J. B. Lippincott,**
1960. (9–12)
Narrated by Scout Finch, an eight-year-old girl, the story chronicles
the early stirrings of civil rights activities, as played out in the
Southern town of Maycomb in the 1930s. Scout's father, Atticus,
refuses to be intimidated by the threats of prejudiced neighbors, and
defends a black man who is falsely accused of raping a white
woman. Through their father's courageous actions, Scout and her
brother learn that they are responsible not only for themselves but
also their fellowmen.

Applications: Values:
Social Studies–Race relations,   Courage, Integrity,
  The South   Family unity

Lenski, Lois (author and illustrator), *Strawberry Girl*. J. B. Lippincott, 1945. (5–8). Newbery Medal
This author demonstrated great interest in helping children to see beyond their own small world and to learn tolerance for people different from themselves. *Strawberry Girl*, which shows us the life of the "Crackers" of Florida in the 1940s, is part of a Regional America series Lenski wrote to achieve her goal. Other titles include *Blue Ridge Billy, Cotton Patch*, and *Shoo-Fly Girl.*

Applications: Values:
Social Studies–Florida, Cultural   Determination,
  awareness   Tolerance, Family unity
Language Arts–Introduction to
  series

Levitin, Sonia, *The Return*. Fawcett, 1988. (9–12)
Desta, an Ethiopian Jew, is forced to flee her native land because of growing persecution by her countrymen. Somehow she must cross the Sudan with her brother and sister to reach the Promised Land of Israel. The reader travels with the small band of refugees as they face the dangers and privations of the desert.

Applications: Values:
History–Ethiopia, Africa, Jews   Faith, Courage,
Psychology–Survival   Family unity

Lewis, Elizabeth, *Young Fu of the Upper Yangtze*. Illustrated by Ed Young. Holt, Rinehart, Winston, 1932. (9–12) Newbery Medal
Young Fu becomes an apprentice to a coppersmith of Chungking during the turbulent 1920s in China. As his country grapples with political upheaval without, Young Fu struggles with issues of honesty and responsibility within as he comes of age. This is a story rich in drama, history, and humor.

Applications: Values:
History–China   Honesty, Dependability,
Psychology–Decision making   Family unity

Lowry, Lois, *Number the Stars.* Bantam, 1989. (4–7) Newbery Medal
When Nazi occupation threatened the Jewish people in Denmark, their friends often took great risks to protect the victimized race. This is a wonderful story of courage, friendship, and faith as daring steps were taken to get one Jewish family to the safety of Sweden.

Applications:	Values:
Social Studies–Jews, World War II	Courage,
Language Arts–Journaling,	Religious freedom,
Dramatization	Ethnic respect

Martin, Bill, and John Archambault, *Knots on a Counting Rope.* Illustrated by Ted Rand. Henry Holt, 1987. (K–4)
Grandfather was there when Boy-Strength-of-Blue-Horses was born. As he grows, grandfather teaches him to ride horses and to find his way through the desert, giving him wisdom, love, and support as he learns to live with his blindness.

Applications:	Values:
Social Studies–Indians of North America	Courage, Love, Independence
Health–Blindness	
Psychology–Cross-generational relationships	

Mathis, Sharon Bell, *The Hundred Penny Box.* Illustrated by Leo and Diane Dillon. Viking, 1975. (3–6) Newbery Honor
Great-great-aunt Lew has a box containing one penny for each year she has lived. That makes one hundred pennies in all. When his mother threatens to throw away the unsightly box in which the pennies are housed, Michael comes to his Aunt Lew's defense.

Applications:	Values:
Psychology–Cross-generational relationships	Understanding, Patience
Language Arts–Reading aloud	
Mathematics–Counting	

Mathis, Sharon Bell, *Sidewalk Story*. Illustrated by Leo Carty. Trumpet Club, 1971.
When Lilly Etta sees her friend's furniture being carried out of the apartment building across the street, she knows that the family is being evicted from their home, and their belongings will be left on the sidewalk for anyone to have. Although the grown-ups around her feel nothing can be done, Lilly Etta determines that her friends will not lose their home without a fight.

Applications:
Language Arts–Creative writing
Social Studies–Poverty,
  Homelessness

Values:
Initiative, Compassion,
Friendship

McCully, Emily Arnold (author and illustrator), *Mirette on the High Wire*. Putnam, 1992. (K–4) Caldecott Medal
When Mirette, a young girl who helps her mother run a theatrical boardinghouse in Paris, watches their new boarder crossing the courtyard on air, she is entranced. She too wants to walk the wire. With Bellini's instruction, she perfects the skill and is able to help him overcome his own fears. The illustrations of Paris have the flavor of the work of Toulouse-Lautrec.

Applications:
Social Studies–France
Psychology–Overcoming fear

Values:
Courage, Determination,
Compassion, Friendship

McKissack, Patricia, *Flossie and the Fox*. Illustrated by Rachel Isadora. Dial Books, 1986. (K–4)
The author reaches back into her childhood memories to share a story told by her grandfather about a resourceful little girl and a fox that tries hard to prove that he is indeed a fox. By the time he has proven himself, Flossie has accomplished her task and has outwitted the animal known for being sly.

Applications:
Language Arts–Storytelling,
  Folktales, Reading readiness

Values:
Self–reliance, Courage,
Humor

Mitchell, Margaret King, *Uncle Jed's Barbershop.*
Illustrated by James Ransome. Simon & Schuster, 1993.
(K–4)
In recounting the story of Uncle Jed, a traveling black barber living
in the segregated South of the 1920s, Margaret Mitchell has created
a book of rare beauty, which is well-supported by the illustrations
of James Ransome. Facing many setbacks with grace, Uncle Jed is
finally able to open his own shiny new barbershop.

Applications: Values:
Psychology–Value of dreams   Perseverance,
Social Studies–Race relations,   Unselfish ness
  The Great Depression

Myers, Walter Dean, *Scorpions.* **Harper Keypoint, 1988.**
(5–8) Newbery Honor
Jamal's brother is in jail for a gang-related offense. During his
absence, Jamal is thought to be the leader of the gang, the
Scorpions. Jamal has some definite feelings about what should or
should not be done by the gang, and by him–leader or not. He sees
that the only way he can earn the respect of fellow gang members,
is to carry a gun–which he does not want to do. This little book
gives an intimate and realistic view of a close-knit family unit trying
to survive the pressures of ghetto life.

Applications: Values:
Psychology–Problem solving,   Friendship, Loyalty
  Divided families

Namioka, Lensey, *Yang the Youngest and His Terrible*
Ear. **Illustrated by Kees DeKiefte. Dell, 1992. (5–8)**
The youngest member of this musically talented Chinese-American
family, Yang has no ear for music. No matter how many hours he
must practice, his skills do not improve. It is difficult for his father,
who teaches violin, to understand that Yang's talents lie in another
direction. Namioka tells her story with humor and sensitivity.

Applications: Values:
Social Studies–Cultural awareness   Obedience,
Music   Self-respect

O'Dell, Scott, *Island of the Blue Dolphins.* **Houghton Mifflin, 1960. (6–12) Newbery Award**
This is a story of courage and survival accomplished alone. When her tribe leaves, Karana remains on their island without company for eighteen years. To survive, she must overcome superstitious taboos and become totally self-sufficient. Although she keeps watch for a boat to rescue her, she learns how to provide food, clothing, and shelter for herself.

Applications:	Values:
Language Arts–Compare to other survival stories	Courage, Survival, Coping, Ingenuity
History–Pacific Indian tribes	

Phillips, Michael, and Judith Pella, *The Heather Hills of Stonewycke.* **Bethany House, 1985. (9–12)**
Phillips and Pella tell the story of Stonewycke, the inheritance of Atlanta Duncan who is descended from the aristocratic Scottish family of Ramsey. Written in the gothic tradition, with an evil conspiracy, a secret excavation, and a mysterious murder, this novel tells of Atlanta's fight to keep the estate together and of her daughter Margaret's search for identity. Other titles in the trilogy include *Flight From Stonewycke* and *Lady of Stonewycke.*

Applications:	Values:
History–Scotland	Courage, Family Heritage

Polacco, Patricia (author and illustrator), *Chicken Sunday.* **Putnam, 1992. (K–4)**
Two African-American children wish to buy a special Easter hat for their grandmother, Miss Eula. With the help of a Russian immigrant girl who is their friend, they make and sell enough "Pysanky" eggs to buy the hat. Patricia Polacco's illustrations help tell the story in a charming manner.

Applications:	Values:
Art–Decorate Pysanky eggs, Decorate hats and caps	Cooperation, Friendship
Social Studies–Cultural awareness	

Polacco, Patricia (author and illustrator), *Just Plain Fancy.* **Trumpet Club, 1990. (K–3)**
Growing up among the "plain folk" in Lancaster County, Pennsylvania, Naomi wishes–just once–to have something fancy. Her wish is granted in a most unusual way. Patricia Polacco's wonderfully expressive illustrations give the reader a glimpse into Amish society.

Applications: Values:
Social Studies–Amish   Dependability
Art–Draw something fancy

Polacco, Patricia (author and illustrator), *Pink and Say.* **Philomel, 1994. (4–8)**
Wounded in battle, Sheldon Russell Curtis is left for dead in a Georgia pasture. There he is found by Pinkus Aylee, a black Union soldier, who takes him to his mother's cabin for care. When they attempt to return to their units they are caught by Confederate soldiers. In sharing with her readers a story that has been passed down the generations of her family, Patricia Polacco has created a simple book of overwhelming impact.

Applications: Values:
Social Studies–Civil War, Race   Friendship,
  relations   Self-sacrifice

Porter, Connie, *Meet Addy.* **Pleasant Company, 1993. (3–8)**
Addy, her mother, and a baby sister escape from Master Steven's plantation after he sells her father and brother to another slave-holder. With the aid of Miss Caroline, they make their way toward freedom and a new life. Presenting American history as it touched the lives of young girls, the Pleasant Company has made an excellent contribution to children's literature through this engaging heroine.

Applications: Values:
Social Studies–Slavery   Courage,
Language Arts–Introduction to   Family Unity
  The American Girl series

Potok, Chaim, *The Chosen.* Simon & Schuster, 1967. (9–12)
Two Jewish boys growing up in Brooklyn live in different worlds. Reuben is the Americanized son of a Zionist professor. Danny, a brilliant scholar, is the son of a leader in the ultra-conservative Hasidic sect. Growing through their years of spiritual and intellectual maturation, they learn to appreciate each other's backgrounds. Potok lends to his writing an understanding of human nature and of the Jewish experience in America.

Applications: Values:
History–Jews in the United States,   Respect,
  Cultural awareness   Tolerance
Psychology–Self-acceptance

Richter, Conrad, *The Light in the Forest.* Knopf, 1966. (9–12)
Kidnapped and adopted by the Lenape Indian tribe as a young child, True Son is recaptured as a teenager and returned to his white family. By that age, True Son views himself as an Indian and has great difficultry adapting to this new role. Unfortunately, on his way to rejoin his foster parents, he warns white occupants of a river boat that Indians are lying in ambush and the tribe will no longer accept him.

Applications: Values:
History–Indians in the United   Cultural appreciation
  States, Race relations
Psychology–Orphans, Self-
  acceptance

Robbins, Charlemae Hill, *They Showed the Way.* Thomas Y. Crowell, 1964. (5–8)
The forty persons of distinction included in this volume triumphed over prejudice and discrimination to excel in fields such as law, medicine, science, and the arts. The short vignettes presented should whet appetites to learn more about these inspiring Americans.

Applications: Values:
History–Cultural awareness   Perseverance, Integrity,
Psychology–Heroes   Excellence

Rue, Nancy N., *Home by Another Way.* **Crossway Books, 1991. (9–12)**
Told from the first-person perspective, this young adult novel reveals the dreams of fifteen-year-old Olympic hopeful, Josh Daniels, a young man who lives for diving. The location of the pool where his coach is employed forces Josh to walk several blocks through a Vietnamese neighborhood where he meets a youngster named Phong. This personal encounter brings lasting changes into his life.

Applications:	Values:
Language Arts–Journaling, Predicting	Self-understanding
History–Cultural awareness	

Rylant, Cynthia, *The Relatives Came.* **Illustrated by Stephen Gammell. Bradbury Press, 1985. (1–5) Caldecott Honor**
Rylant's humorous book relates the journey of a car full of rural relatives traveling to another country setting for a summer visit. Gammell's action-filled illustrations make this oversized book a real winner. Much is included of the work, play, and rest of a rural family in the 1940s.

Applications:	Values:
Language Arts–Reading aloud	Family life, Humor,
Social Studies–Appalachia	Helpfulness
Psychology–Family	

Rylant, Cynthia, *When I Was Young in the Mountains.* **Illustrated by Drane Goode. E.P. Dutton, 1982. (1–5) Caldecott Honor**
Growing up in the mountains is pictured here as a warm and wonderful experience. Rylant describes daily life, religion, and recreation with such charm that she causes the reader to smile with a tear in her eye.

Applications:	Values:
Social Studies–Genealogy Appalachia	Appreciation of heritage

Say, Allen, *Grandfather's Journey*. Houghton Mifflin, 1993. (K–4) Caldecott Medal
A young Japanese American tells of his grandfather's journey to America, a trip which he later repeats himself. He recounts the feeling of being torn by a love for two different countries and the homesickness that comes as a result. With his eloquent pictures, Allen Say has created a work of great beauty.

Applications: Values:
History–Immigration, Japan   Cultural appreciation,
Psychology–Cross-generational   Family unity, Heritage
  relations, Homesickness

Sperry, Armstrong, *Call It Courage*. Macmillan, 1940. (5–8) Newbery Medal
Determined to conquer his fear of the sea that took his mother's life, twelve-year-old Mafatu sets off in a small canoe with his dog, Uri, and his sea gull, Kivi, to find islands to the south of his own island of Hikueru. This classic tale of survival is filled with heart-stopping adventure and suspense.

Applications: Values:
Social Studies–Polynesia   Courage, Ingenuity,
  Island life   Determination
Psychology–Survival, Fear

Spyri, Johanna, *Heidi*. Putnam Publishing Group, 1880, 1981. (5–8)
In the beautiful Alps of Switzerland, Heidi's need for love and care transforms her grandfather from a bitter, lonely man to a person able to give and receive. When Heidi is taken away by her aunt to be companion to a wealthy young crippled girl, she is able to overcome her homesickness for her grandfather to bring joy and hope to others.

Applications: Values:
Social Studies–Switzerland   Kindness, Love,
Psychology–Orphans,   Faithfulness
  Cross-generational relationships,
  Single parents, Physical handicaps

Taylor, Mildred, *Roll of Thunder, Hear My Cry*. Dial Press, 1976. **(9–12) Newbery Medal**
Living in Mississippi during the Depression, the Logan family struggles to maintain their pride and independence in the face of great financial struggle and deep racial prejudice. Cassie Logan's story is one of warm family love amid terrifying events. It is an uncomfortable, but necessary and unforgettable, book.

Applications:	Values:
Social Studies–Race relations,	Honor, Courage,
The Great Depression	Family unity

Taylor, Sydney, *All-Of-A-Kind Family*. Illustrated by Helen John. Follett, 1951. (5–8)
A family of Jewish immigrants from Czechoslovakia comes to live on Manhattan's Lower East Side during the 1900s. The five daughters of this active family are firmly but fondly guided by their parents, who pass along to them their Jewish heritage and traditions. This series is continued in *More All-Of-A-Kind Family*.

Applications:	Values:
Social Studies–Immigrations,	Respect, Love,
Jewish life	Cooperation
Language Arts–Compare to	
Little Women	

Turkle, Brinton (author and illustrator), *Thy Friend Obadiah*. Puffin, 1987. (K–4) Caldecott Honor
When one of the seagulls on Nantucket Island becomes attached to young Obadiah, following him everywhere, the little Quaker boy refuses to accept the attention. However, when winter comes and the seagull gets into serious trouble, Obadiah changes his mind and returns the friendship.

Applications:	Values:
Social Studies–Quakers,	Kindness,
New England in the 1700s.	Appreciation of animals
Science–Birds, Seaports	

Voigt, Cynthia, *Come a Stranger.* **Atheneum, 1986.**
(9–12)
Mina Smith is dedicated to ballet and is thrilled at the opportunity
to go to a special ballet school during the summer. She is not
concerned that she is the only Black girl there, and is able to make
friends. The following summer, however, is different, and she has
a painful lesson in prejudice. When a young pastor takes an
interest in helping her through this ordeal, she is able, in turn, to
help him repay an old debt.

Applications: Values:
History–Race relations   Family unity,
                                     Self-acceptance

Williams, Sherley Anne, *Working Cotton.* **Illustrated by**
Carole Byard. Harcourt, 1992. (K–4) Caldecott Honor
Written in dialect, the story evokes images of a migrant laborer's
day in the cotton fields of Fresno. It is a simple, thought-provoking
book written from the viewpoint of Shelan, who is too little to carry
a sack of her own, but piles cotton in the middle of the row for her
mama to collect. In spite of the hardships portrayed, this is a
positive book, full of family love.

Applications: Values:
Social Studies–Migrant labor   Family love,
                                     Work Ethic

Winter, Jeanette (author and illustrator), *Follow the*
Drinking Gourd. **Alfred A. Knopf, 1988. (K–4)**
Peg Leg Joe, a conductor on the Underground Railway, hires out to
plantation owners as a handyman in order to teach slaves a folksong
that contains directions for following a route to freedom in the
North. The title refers to the North Star found at the end of the Big
Dipper, which the slaves used as a guide. The author has
effectively portrayed the dangers and sacrifice faced by the fleeing
slaves and those who helped them.

Applications: Values:
Social Studies–Slavery, The Under-   Courage,
  ground Railroad   Self-sacrifice

Yashima, Taro (author and illustrator), *Crow Boy.*
Viking Press, 1955. **(K–4)** **Caldecott Honor**
A shy little Japanese farm boy from the mountains is shunned at school because he is unlike the other boys and girls. A new teacher finally makes contact with the boy and discovers that he has unique knowledge and talents to share with the class.

Applications: Values:
Social Studies–Japan   Perseverance, Kindness
Psychology–Shyness, Individuality,
   Peer pressure

CHAPTER FIVE

HISTORICAL FICTION

Reading historical fiction can be like listening to grandparents tell about how they lived as children. Through these stories, children can develop a sense of place in their family, their country, and the world. *Waiting for the Evening Star* (Wells), *Yonder* (Johnston), and Anno's *U.S.A.* provide a strong sense of family belonging and the passing–down of land and traditions. Historical fiction can also develop understanding of how our lives have been affected by the actions and decisions of others. Malcolm McPhail, as portrayed in *The Fisherman's Lady* (MacDonald), was one whose destiny was marked by the decisions of others. As his fortunes reversed on his coming of age, he demonstrated an understanding of how his decisions would, in turn, affect the tomorrows of many others.

In true historical fiction, the time period is at the core of the story. The characters portrayed are caught up in the events of the time, reacting to the forces shaping the history of the chosen period. Some of the characters may be people who actually lived, but the major thrust of the work is not a detailing of life events as much as a re-creation of the aura of the time. Paul Revere, Sam Adams, and numerous other Revolutionary War figures appear in *Johnny Tremain* (Forbes), for example, but the thrust of the story is the effect of the rebellion on the life of a young boy pulled into the events. Some stories contain no persons who really lived, but

are simply drawn within the context of the time period, such
as *Sarah Plain and Tall* (MacLachlan) and *Homer Price*
(McCloskey). Historical novels emphasize a number of themes.
Authors such as Laura Ingalls Wilder (*Little House on the
Prairie*), Virginia Sorensen, (*Miracles on Maple Hill*), and
Joan W. Blos (*Gathering of Days*) write of daily domestic
events showing how families worked together to survive
hard times. Emily Bronte, in what is credited as being the
first gothic novel (*Jane Eyre*), and Joan Aiken (*Wolves of
Willoughby Chase*) created suspenseful psychological
thrillers. For fast-paced adventure, *The Scarlet Pimpernel*
(Orczy) and *Trouble River* (Byars), should satisfy. Setting
takes precedence in *All the Places to Love* (MacLachlan),
while character development is the emphasis in *A Tale Of
Two Cities* by Charles Dickens. Titles of social and political
realism, such as *Florian's Gate* (Bunn) and *Year of
Impossible Goodbyes* (Choi), have been included in this
chapter on historical fiction, but most books emphasizing a
strong ethnic heritage can be found in the chapter on
multicultural fiction.

No matter what the theme, historical novels are a
skillful blending of fact and fiction, information and
imagination. Accurate details of transportation, food, clothing, housing, and societal attitudes must fit the time and
place of the setting as a natural extension of the text. In
stories such as *The Bronze Bow* (Speare), set during the
Roman occupation of Israel, the author must often provide
more background information for the reader than is
demanded in contemporary works. While this information
is essential to the understanding of the story, the author is
faced with the challenge of making these descriptions flow
easily with the plot, for readers are primarily interested in a
good story.

Aiken, Joan, *The Wolves of Willoughby Chase.* **Dell, 1962. (5–8)**
When their parents depart on a sea voyage, Bonnie and Sylvia are left in the care of cruel Miss Slighcarp, who sets out to make Willoughby Chase her own. Sent away to an orphan school, the girls enlist the aid of Simon the gooseboy to escape and thwart the plans of the evil Miss Slighcarp. Aiken's works are full of drama, exaggeration, and imagination.

Applications: Values:
Social Studies–Victorian Life   Courage,
Language Arts–Mysteries   Imagination.

Alcott, Louisa May, *Little Women.* **Puffin, 1868, 1988. (9–12)**
Although set during the Civil War, the themes developed by Alcott are universal. In the absence of their father who is at war, the daughters are taught and nurtured by their mother as they grow into thoughtful and loving young women. In spite of the many difficulties they experience, the daughters are joyful and refreshing.

Applications: Values:
Language Arts–Unit on Alcott,   Honesty, Love,
  Compare to *All-of-a-Kind Family*   Family unity,
Social Studies–Civil War   Kindness
Psychology–Single parent
  families

Anno, Mitsumasa, *Anno's U.S.A.* **Philomel Books, 1992. (K–6)**
Anno pictures America of the past and the present, portraying big cities, small towns, and wide countryside. Incorporating characters from other books, elements of famous paintings, and historical figures, the artist has created a wordless book full of stories.

Applications: Values:
Social Studies–United States   Imagination,
                                       Appreciation of nature

Austen, Jane, *Pride and Prejudice.* **Dodd, Mead, 1813, 1945. (9–12)**
In her novel of courtship, Jane Austen highlights the social tensions of nineteenth-century England, when English society lived by a strict code of behavior. The battle of wits between Darcy and Elizabeth demonstrates the pride and prejudices of English society and points out the value of humanity versus the pretensions of social position.

Applications: Values:
Language Arts–Satire   Wit, Family unity
History–England

Beatty, Patricia, *Jayhawker.* **Morrow, 1991. (5–8)**
After his abolitionist father is killed during a raid on a slaveholders' plantation, Lije agrees to live with a group of Southern bush-whackers in order to work as a spy for the Union. Lije soon realizes what a dangerous role he is playing in events that are driving the country to war.

Applications: Values:
History–Civil War, Slavery,   Courage, Ingenuity,
  Contrast with *Shades of Gray*   Coping with difficulty
Psychology–Decision making,
  Loss of father

Blos, Joan W., *A Gathering of Days.* **Scribners, 1979. (5–12) Newbery Medal**
Written in diary form, this story pictures daily routines in the life of a thirteen-year-old girl in eighteenth-century New England. Her descriptions of adjusting to a stepmother, grieving over the death of a dear friend, and aiding a fugitive slave evoke issues that are still relevant today.

Applications: Values:
Language Arts–Compare to *Calico*   Courage, Friendship,
  Bush, Journal writing   Work ethic
History–Colonial life
Psychology–Stepparents

Brink, Carol Ryrie, *Caddie Woodlawn.* **Aladdin, 1935, 1990 (5–8) Newbery Medal**
Caddie, an eleven-year-old tomboy living on a Wisconsin farm in the 1860s, would rather plow the fields and hunt with her brothers than sew and cook with her mother. The adventuresome spirit of this young pioneer girl brings both trial and blessing to her family.

Applications:
Language Arts–Compare to
  The Courage of Sarah Noble
History–Frontier and pioneer life
Psychology–Siblings

Values:
Honesty, Courage,
Kindness, Loyalty,
Family unity

Bronte, Charlotte, *Jane Eyre.* **Grossett and Dunlop, 1847, 1983. (9–12)**
Orphaned in early childhood, shy, ordinary eighteen-year-old Jane comes to Thornfield as governess for the ward of Mr. Rochester, a rude and melancholy man. As Jane is gradually made aware of mystery and danger in the house, she becomes enmeshed in twists and turns of plot which bring her, in the end, to great joy.

Applications:
History–Victorian life, Treatment
  of mentally ill
Psychology–Orphans

Values:
Responsibility, Love,
Endurance, Forgiveness

Bulla, Clyde Robert, *A Lion to Guard Us.* **Harper Collins, 1981. (5–8)**
The Freebold children make an ocean voyage to the new Virginia colony in 1609 to find the father who has gone before them. Their only tangible link to him is the brass lion door knocker from their home in England. When some of their shipmates believe that the knocker is made of gold, the children face more challenges than the sea.

Applications:
History–Immigration,
  Frontier and pioneer life
Language Arts–Sea stories

Values:
Family love, Courage,
Perseverance

Bunn, T. Davis, *Florian's Gate.* **Bethany House, 1993. (10–12)**
Those seeking an understanding of the struggles of modern–day Eastern Europe can find illumination in this book by T. Davis Bunn. Supported by an absorbing plot, the story tells of a man coming to grips with faith in the midst of a chaotic society.

Applications:
Language Arts–Introduction to
   series including *The Amber Room*
   and *Winter Palace*
History–Eastern Europe, Poland

Values:
Faithfulness, Humility,
Compassion

Burnett, Frances Hodgson, *The Little Princess.* **HarperCollins Children's Books, 1905, 1963. (5–8)**
Sara is brought to London from India by her wealthy father for the purpose of attending boarding school. When word of her father's death and financial ruin reach the headmistress, Sara's position rapidly deteriorates. In spite of the poor treatment she receives, Sara acts with kindness and consideration for those less fortunate.

Applications:
Social Studies–England
Psychology–Death of parent,
   Peer pressure

Values:
Self-control, Kindness
Obedience, Humility

Byars, Betsy, *Trouble River.* **Viking, 1969. (5–8)**
Dewey's father takes his mother into town to have her baby, leaving Dewey and his grandmother alone in their prairie cabin. When hostile Indians come, they use the raft that Dewey has secretly built to escape down the river. Not only does this young man display courage in facing the dangers of the river, he has unswerving patience in dealing with his cranky grandmother.

Applications:
Language Arts–Compare with
   Caddie Woodlawn
History–Frontier and pioneer life
Psychology–Survival

Values:
Courage, Ingenuity,
Perseverance,
Cross-generational
respect

Caldwell, Taylor, *Dear and Glorious Physician.* **Double-day, 1959. (9–12)**
Lucanus, the Greek, stepson to the Roman governor of Antioch, became one of the great physicians of the ancient world. During his travels through the Mediterranean region he learns of the life of Christ and finds in him the answer to his heart's desires.

Applications:	Values:
History–Roman Empire,	Self-sacrifice,
Israel	Perseverance,
Language Arts–Biography	Dedication

Choi, Sook Nyul, *Year of Impossible Goodbyes.* **Dell, 1991. (9–12)**
Oppressed by the cruelties of the Japanese military occupying Korea in 1945, Sookan's family refuses to allow their spirits to be broken. At the end of the war, when the Communist troops take control of North Korea, the family realizes their hope for freedom lies in escape to the south.

Applications:	Values:
History–Korea	Loyalty, Family,
Language Arts–Compare to	Courage,
House of Sixty Fathers	Determination
Psychology–Survival	

Cleaver, Vera and Bill, *Where the Lilies Bloom.* **Scholastic, 1969, 1974. (7–12)**
At her father's death, Mary Call promises she will keep the family together without taking charity, no matter how difficult the circumstances. The spunk that she displays in attempting to keep her promise makes her a true heroine.

Applications:	Values:
History–Appalachian mountains	Family unity, Love,
Science–Herb gathering	Courage, Ingenuity
Psychology–Survival as orphans,	
Compare to *Dicey's Song*	

Cooper, James Fenimore, *The Last of the Mohicans.*
Bantam, 1826, 1982. (9–12)
Based on the surrender of Fort William Henry in 1757, this book
chronicles the struggle for control by the French, English, and
various Indian tribes. Natty Bumppo and the loyal Chingachgook,
along with strong and noble Uncas, remain central characters in this
most popular of the *Leather-Stocking Tales.*

Applications: Values:
History–French and Indian War,   Courage, Loyalty
   Frontier and pioneer life,
   Indians of North America,
   New York State

Costain, Thomas, *The Silver Chalice.* **Doubleday, 1952.**
(9–12)
Basil of Antioch, a skilled artisan, is bought from slavery to craft
the covering for a silver cup that is used by Christ at the Last
Supper. His project takes him through the spectacular capitals of
the ancient world, as he braves many perils in his search for truth.

Applications: Values:
History–Ancient world,   Courage, Love,
   Rome, Biblical history   Perseverance

Crane, Stephen, *The Red Badge of Courage.* **Vintage,**
1895, 1990. (9–12)
A young soldier's romantic dreams of war are shattered after
experiencing the horrors of his first Civil War battle. The inner
conflict between fear and courage that rages within the boy is as
intense as the battles that swirl around him. Loyalty to his fellow
soldiers enables him to conquer his fears and take his place at their
side.

Applications: Values:
History–Civil War   Courage, Loyalty
Literature–Symbolism, Stream
   of consciousness

Crofford, Emily, *A Place to Belong*. Carolrhoda, 1994. (5–9)

Talmadge's family must deal with many difficult struggles during the Great Depression including the loss of their Tennessee farm and his sister Roseanne's bout with infantile paralysis. Through each trial, their love and mutual respect bring them closer together.

Applications:
History–The Great Depression
Health–Physical handicaps
Psychology–Overcoming adversity

Values:
Family unity, Respect,

deAngeli, Marguerite (author and illustrator), *The Door in the Wall*. Scholastic Press, 1949, 1984. (4–8) Newbery Award

Living in London during the period of the Black Death while his parents are away in service to the king, Robin is deserted by all the family servants when he too becomes ill. Rescued from his plight by a friar who cares for him and helps him to adjust to the lameness that results from his illness, Robin later becomes a hero.

Applications:
Social Studies–Middle Ages
Literature–Reading aloud
Health–Physical handicaps,
   Research cause of Black Death

Values:
Kindness, Courage

dePaola, Tomie (author and illustrator), *The Clown of God*. Harcourt Brace Jovanovich, 1978 (1–adult)

dePaola retells an old Italian folktale about a youthful beggar who gains much success by becoming a juggler. With age, however, the juggler loses his touch and becomes the object of scorn. On Christmas Eve, he takes refuge from this ridicule in a church and gives the final performance of his life, as an act of devotion to the child held in Mary's arms. This selfless act results in a miracle.

Applications:
History–Middle Ages, Italy
Language Arts–Reading aloud,
   Storytelling

Values:
Sacrifice, Love,
Giving

Dickens, Charles, *A Tale of Two Cities*. Harper Collins, 1859, 1992 (9–12)

In this story, Dickens recreates the atmosphere of fear and insanity that overshadowed the underlying hope and stated ideals of the French Revolution as The Committee of Public Safety ruled the streets, sending aristocrat and peasant alike to the guillotine. Themes of vengeance, injustice, and the ultimate sacrifice of giving one's life for another are developed throughout the book.

Applications:	Values:
History– French Revolution	Self–sacrifice, Mercy,
Language Arts–Compare to other works by Charles Dickens	Courage

Dodge, Mary Mapes, *Hans Brinker; or, The Silver Skates*. Puffin Books, 1865, 1985. (9–12)

Reduced to poverty after their husband and father receives a severe head injury, this Dutch mother and her two children struggle against desperate poverty. The children do what they can to supply the needs of the family and to care for their father, and in the end their loyalty and diligence are well rewarded. Exciting scenes are built around the skating skill of the children.

Applications:	Values:
History–Holland	Compassion, Patience,
Language Arts–Gifted readers Compare to *A Wheel on the School*	Diligence, Faith

Douglas, Lloyd, *The Robe*. Houghton Mifflin, 1942. (9–12)

Marcellus, the young Roman soldier placed in charge of the crucifixion of Jesus, is among those who cast lots for his robe. When the lot falls to him, Marcellus becomes obsessed with finding out the true identity of Jesus.

Applications:	Values:
History–Roman civilization, Middle East	Faith, Determination

Doyle, Sir Arthur Conan, *The Adventures of Sherlock Holmes.* **Viking Penguin, 1892, 1981. (7–12)**
Sherlock Holmes remains, even today, the ultimate example of the master detective. His cases challenge readers to use their best deductive abilities to solve mysteries that baffle even Scotland Yard. Curious readers are also introduced to countless areas of science and history to entice them into further inquiry.

Applications:
Language Arts–Mystery,
  Recreational reading
History–England

Values:
Logical thinking,
Perseverance

Dumas, Alexander, *The Count of Monte Cristo.* **New American Library, 1892, 1988. (9–12)**
A classic adventure story with fast–paced action, this story relates Edmond Dantes quest to track down the men who had imprisoned him in the Chateau D'If. Though the villains are found and justly punished, Dantes learns that forgiveness brings true healing in the face of injustice.

Applications:
History–France

Values:
Patience, Forgiveness,
Humility

Edmonds, Walter D. *Drums along the Mohawk.* **Bantam, 1936, 1988. (9–12)**
Set in the Mohawk Valley during the American Revolution, this tale portrays vividly the danger and privation endured by frontier pioneers. Edmonds presents a realistic picture, as his heroes are allowed to make human mistakes and their Indian and Tory enemies display both bravery and determination. Not easy reading, this story is, nonetheless worthwhile for the gifted young person.

Applications:
History–United States Revolution,
  Frontier and pioneer life
Literature–For gifted readers

Values:
Courage, Diligence

Eliot, George, *Silas Marner.* **Dutton, 1861, 1960.** **(9–12)**
Through a series of misfortunes, Silas comes to live alone in a
cottage outside of Raveloe, England, a bitter, lonely man. On New
Year's Eve, however, a little girl with golden hair, newly orphaned
by the tragic death of her mother, wanders into his cottage. Eppie,
as Silas calls her, claims his complete devotion and rekindles his
interest in life and love.

Applications:	Values:
History–England in 1860s	Family love, Self-
Psychology–Orphans	sacrifice

Enright, Elizabeth (author and illustrator), *Thimble
Summer,* **Holt, Rinehart and Winston, 1966.** **(4–6)**
Newbery Award
The summer that Garnet finds a silver thimble in the bend of the
creek turns out to be a magic year full of the adventures of growing
up. Those who believe that living on a farm is dull should read this
book.

Applications:	Values:
Social Studies–Farm life	Work ethic,
	Family unity

Field, Rachel, *Calico Bush.* **Macmillan, 1931.** **(9–12)**
Newbery Honor Book
Orphaned by the death of her grandmother and uncle, Marguerite
Ledoux, a thirteen-year-old French girl, is "bound-out" to Joel and
Dolly Sargent, an English family, who take her with them to the
edge of the Maine wilderness. Together they share the hardships,
dangers, and blessings of pioneer life as they live through the first
bitter winter and hopeful spring. The courage and ingenuity that
Maggie displays builds the Sargents' trust in her and they all come
to a growing respect and affection for each other.

Applications:	Values:
History–Colonial life, Cultural	Courage, Work ethic,
awareness	Unselfishness
Language arts–Compare to *A*	
Gathering of Days	

Fleischman, Sid, *The Whipping Boy*. Greenwillow Books, 1986. (4–8) **Newbery Award**
Since no one is allowed to punish the prince, a young orphan named Jemmy is taken from the streets to serve as a whipping boy whenever the prince does something wrong. When Prince Brat runs away taking Jemmy with him, he finds adventure, suspense, and the reality that the outside world is not so tolerant of his bad behavior.

Applications:
Language Arts–Reluctant readers,
  For advanced readers use *The Prince and the Pauper* by Mark Twain
Social Studies–Middle Ages

Values:
Unselfishness, Humor, Self-discipline

Forbes, Esther, *Johnny Tremain*. Houghton Mifflin, 1943. (6–12) **Newbery Medal**
When a crippling accident puts an end to Johnny's apprenticeship to a silversmith, he discovers a new role as messenger for the Sons of Liberty, a group of colonists who want separation from English rule. Johnny struggles with his handicap and pride as he takes part in the nation's struggle for independence.

Applications:
History–American Revolution
Health–Physical handicaps

Values:
Courage, Humility, Loyalty

Fritz, Jean, *Shh! We're Writing the Constitution*. Illustrated by Tomie dePaola. Putnam's Sons, 1987. (3–8)
The business of government is made real and understandable to children by author Jean Fritz. Not only are the issues that face the infant American nation presented in this volume, but also the personalities and everyday life of the delegates. Tomie de Paola's illustrations add a light touch.

Applications:
Social Studies–Government,
  United States Constitution

Values:
Cooperation, Perseverance

Gardiner, John Reynolds, *Stone Fox.* **Trumpet Book Club, 1980. (4–8)**
When the state of Wyoming threatens to take away their farm for nonpayment of taxes, Willy's grandfather loses his will to live. Willy determines to win the $500 needed by competing in the National Sled Dog Races. To win, he must compete against the best dogsled racers in the country–including the Indian, Stone Fox.

Applications:	Values:
Social Studies–Wyoming	Determination,
Psychology–Cross-generational	Courage, Endurance,
relations, Compare to *Trouble*	Love
River	

Garfield, Leon, *Fair's Fair.* **Illustrated by S. D. Schindler, Doubleday, 1981. (1–4)**
When Jackson, a homeless, ragged orphan shares his pie with a hungry black dog, he finds a key around the animal's neck. Setting out to find the owner of the dog and the key, he discovers greater adventure than anticipated and proves the generosity of his own heart.

Applications:	Values:
Social Studies–England	Honesty, Generosity,
Psychology–Orphans, Homelessness	Industry
Christmas	

Gipson, Fred, *Old Yeller.* **Harper, 1956, 1990. (5–8)**
When a big, ugly, yellow dog shows up at their snug Texas cabin, stealing a whole side of pork, fourteen-year-old Travis wants to chase him away. But when his Pa joins a cattle drive, leaving the boy with the awesome responsibility of care for his Ma, his brother, and the farm, Travis comes to depend on the dog as a helper and friend.

Applications:	Values:
History–Frontier life, Texas	Courage, Cooperation,
Language Arts–Dog stories	Responsibility

Gray, Elizabeth Janet, *Adam of the Road.* **Viking, 1942.**
(5–8) Newbery Award
Adam, whose minstrel father goes from castle to town, entertaining
kings and commoners alike, is separated from his horse, his red
spaniel, and his father by the dishonest Janki. As Adam sets out to
make things right, the reader learns much about the customs, dress,
standards of living, food, and mores of the time.

Applications: Values:
Language Arts–Dramatization,   Courage, Survival,
  Compare to *A Door in the Wall*   Perseverance, Self-
History–Middle Ages   reliance, Family unity

Hall, Donald, *The Ox-Cart Man.* **Illustrated by Barbara**
Cooney. Viking, 1979. (K–3) Caldecott Medal
A New England farmer packs his cart full of goods that he and his
family have made over the winter to sell at the Portsmouth Market.
With the coins from his sales, he then buys provision for the
coming year and returns home. In this simple story, Hall has
captured the heart of farm life in sixteenth-century America.

Applications: Values:
Social Studies–Colonial life,   Stewardship, Family,
 Language Arts–Prereading skills,   Cooperation
  Sequencing, Prediction

Hays, Wilma Pitchford, *Trouble at Otter Creek.* **Xerox**
Education, 1978. (3–8)
After her husband's death, Ann Story takes her five children to live
in the cabin he built for them in the Vermont wilderness. Together
they brave wild animals, hostile Indians and Yorkers who contest
their right to own the land. In this and other titles, Wilma Pitchford
Hayes has effectively portrayed episodes of American history in
stories that primary students can understand.

Applications: Values:
Social Studies–Frontier life,   Courage, Family unity
 Vermont, Green Mountain Men

Henderson, Lois T., and Harold Ivan Smith. *Priscilla and Aquila.* **Harper & Row, 1985.** (8–12)
In a series of novels based on the lives of Biblical characters, Lois Henderson has succeeded in adding color and texture to the fabric of historical fact. With the help of cowriter Harold Smith, this particular novel follows Priscilla and Aquila as they flee Rome to Greece, where they meet the apostle Paul. Joining themselves to his ministry, they endure the adversity and persecution which marked his life.

Applications:	Values:
History–Israel, Jewish heritage	Faith, Commitment
Psychology–Persecution, Marriage, Women's role	

Hoff, B. J., *Song of the Silent Harp.* **Bethany House, 1991.** (9–12)
In the 1800s, the Irish Potato Famine ravaged villages already suffering under merciless absentee English landlords. Throughout this devastating period, the Kavanagh family survives because of their love for each other, their commitment to faith, and the help of the rebel poet, Morgan Fitzgerald. This is volume 1 of the Emerald Ballad series.

Applications:	Values:
History–Ireland, Immigration	Faithfulness, Self–
Psychology–Survival	sacrifice

Holm, Anne, *North to Freedom.* **Harcourt Brace, 1963.** (6–12)
David makes his way across Europe after escaping from the fear and want of the concentration camp where he had been born. His trip is not only full of danger, but of the new experiences of seeing life outside captivity for the first time. David is a winsome hero who meets his challenges with courage and honesty.

Applications:	Values:
History–World War II, Refugees	Courage, Freedom
Psychology–Adjustment to new world	

Hunt, Irene, *Across Five Aprils.* Berkeley Press, 1987. (5–8)

Hunt has created a sensitive portrayal of an adolescent boy who lives during the time of the Civil War. As his brothers leave to join the fight, he is left on the family farm in southern Illinois. Through letters his brothers write home, however, he comes to an understanding of the war and to some resolution of the conflicts caused by living in a border state.

Applications:
History–Civil War
Psychology–Adolescence, Resolution of divided loyalties

Values:
Family love, Reliability

Jackson, Dave and Neta, *The Bandit of Ashley Downs.* Bethany House, 1993. (3–6)

Twelve–year–old Curly Roddy is an orphan living on the streets of London in the 1870s. When he is caught trying to rob a carriage, he is sent to an orphanage operated by a man named George Mueller. It is here that Curly's life takes a turn for the better.

Applications:
History–England, Victorian life
Psychology–Orphans

Values:
Faith, Integrity,
Compassion

Johnson, Lois Walfrid, *Trouble at Wildriver.* Bethany House, 1991. (4–8)

In Wisconsin in 1907, Kate and her friends discover a timber swindler while visiting their Indian friend Joe. They suspect that Kate's uncle, newly arrived from Sweden, may be involved. This fifth book in the Adventures in the Northwoods series, builds suspense from the first chapter.

Applications:
History–Wisconsin, Native Americans, Swedes in the U.S.
Science–Logging
Language Arts–Foreshadowing, Mystery

Values:
Courage, Family unity

Johnston, Tony, *Yonder.* Illustrated by Lloyd Bloom. Dial, 1991. (K–4)
Yonder is a touching portrayal of a frontier farming family as it grows through the generations, building a true family homestead.

Applications:
Social Studies–Rural life
Science–Seasons
Art–Appreciation of work of
   Lloyd Bloom

Values:
Family life, Love,
Perseverance

Keith, Harold, *Rifles for Watie.* Thomas Y. Crowell, 1957. (5–12) Newbery Award
Jefferson Davis Bussey, a young Union soldier, is sent behind Confederate lines to spy on Stand Watie, a Cherokee Confederate soldier responsible for stealing rifles from the Union Army. Pretending to be one of them, Jeff learns that many of the enemy are young men just like himself, enduring the hunger, dirt, and weariness of war.

Applications:
History–Civil War
Psychology–Adolescence
Language Arts–Compare to
   Jayhawker

Values:
Courage, Honor,
Self-reliance

Leppard, Lois Gladys, *Mandie and the Cherokee Legend.* Bethany House, 1983. (5–8)
Second in a series about a spunky young heroine living at the turn of the century, this book relates Mandie's adventures in the Cherokee territory of North Carolina. Facing a panther, finding her way out of a cave, outwitting kidnappers–Mandie triumphs over it all, including her own anger and resentment.

Applications:
History–Turn of the century,
   Cultural awareness, Cherokee
Language Arts–Mystery

Values:
Unselfishness,
Forgiveness

**MacDonald, George (adapted by Michael R. Phillips),
The Fisherman's Lady. Bethany House, 1984.** (9–12)
Malcolm McPhail, who has spent most of his youthful years as a
simple Scottish fisherman, is suddenly thrust into a life of intrigue
and danger, haunted by dark secrets of the past. The characters
that people the novels of George MacDonald are real people who
struggle with life's dark forces and emerge victorious.

Applications: Values:
History–Scotland   Integrity, Morality,
Literature–Victorian literature   Good over evil

**MacLachlan, Patricia, *All the Places to Love*. Illustrated
by Mike Wimmer. HarperCollins, 1994.** (K–4)
From the day he is born, Eli is surrounded by family affection and
a love for the beauty of the world. Illustrated with the finely
detailed paintings of Mike Wimmer, this story pays homage to
American farm life and a way of living that values simple pleasures.
Once again Patricia MacLachlan has given readers an unforgettable
book to love.

Applications: Values:
History–Rural life   Family unity
Science–Appreciation of nature
Psychology–Cross-generational
   relations

**MacLachlan, Patricia, *Sarah, Plain and Tall*. Harper &
Row, 1985. (3–8) Newbery Award**
The author demonstrates in this small book that easy reading does
not have to be dull or shallow. This is a tremendously touching
story of children's need for a mother and the individualistic lady
who comes to try the role.

Applications: Values:
Language Arts–Reading aloud   Commitment,
History–Pioneer life   Adjusting to others
Psychology–Stepparents

Magorian, Michelle, *Goodnight, Mr. Tom.* **Harper & Row, 1981. (5–12)**
When bombs threaten the city of London, Willie Beech, timid and scrawny from abuse, is evacuated to the English countryside to live with Mr. Tom, a gruff but kindly old man. Willie blossoms in an atmosphere of friendship and affection until a telegram from his single mother insists he return home. When he does not hear from Willie, Mr. Tom sets out to look for the child he has come to love. This is a powerful story of love overcoming the effects of abusive treatment.

Applications:	Values:
History–World War II, Britain	Love, Security,
Psychology–Child abuse, Single parenting, Cross–generational relationships	Friendship

Marshall, Catherine, *Christy.* **Avon, 1976. (8–12)**
The year is 1912 when young Christy Huddleston leaves the comfortable security of her home to teach at a school sponsored by the American Inland Mission in Cutter Gap, Tennessee. With great love, respect, warmth, and humor, Catherine Marshall recounts her mother's first year of teaching in Appalachia. In 1994 *Christy* was made into a successful television miniseries.

Applications:	Values:
History–Appalachia	Pride, Courage,
Teaching profession	Sacrifice, Love
Sociology–Poverty	

McCloskey, Robert, *Homer Price.* **Viking, 1943. (3–7)**
Whether using his pet skunk to catch robbers, or selling thousands of doughnuts when his uncle's doughnut machine goes haywire, Homer Price handles preposterous situations with common sense and ingenuity. He keeps the reader laughing.

Applications:	Values:
Language Arts–Reading aloud, Dramatization, Creative writing	Humor, Ingenuity

McSwigan, Marie. *Snow Treasure.* **Scholastic, 1986. (5–8)**
When Germans invade their town during World War II, the Norwegian children of Riswyk show great courage as they resist the occupation by helping to smuggle $9 million worth of gold bullion out of the country. Working together, they tie the treasure to their sleds and ride it to the waterfront in full view of the Nazi sentries. There it is loaded in secret onto a ship bound for America and safety.

Applications:	Values:
History–World War II,	Courage, Cooperation
Norway	Ingenuity

Mezek, Karen (author and illustrator), *The Rumpoles and the Barleys.* **Harvest House, 1988. (K–4)**
Eustace and Prunella are haughty, naughty mice who live in the attic of the Rumpole mansion. When their disobedience lands them in a pile of garbage, they are befriended by the Barleys, a family of field mice, who show them the importance of thankfulness and unselfishness.

Applications:	Values:
Language arts–Reading aloud	Obedience, Humility,
	Thankfulness

Montgomery, Lucy Maud, *Anne of Green Gables.* **Putnam, 1915, 1983. (9–12)**
Set on Canada's Prince Edward Island, this story of an orphaned red-haired girl has delighted young readers and adults for years. An impetuous dreamer who loves to read, this extraordinary girl fills the home of spinster Marilla Cuthburt and her bachelor brother Matthew with funny, disastrous adventures as well as abundant love. The saga, continued in *Anne of Avonlea,* was made into a television miniseries which has become a bestselling video.

Applications:	Values:
History–Canada in the early 1900s	Creativity, Humor,
Psychology–Orphans	Family love, Friendship

Morris, Gilbert, *The Reluctant Bridegroom.* **Bethany House, 1987. (9–12)**
Sky Winslow, made resistant to the graces of women from the hurts inflicted by an unfaithful wife, agrees to bring a wagon train of brides to the men of Oregon City. On the long trip West, he finds new and exciting possibilities introduced into his life. This is volume 7 in a series which traces the generations of the Winslow family as it coincides with the history of America.

Applications: Values:
History–United States   Family unity, Courage,
Language Arts–Introduction to   Integrity, Faith
  series

Nixon, Joan Lowry, *A Family Apart.* **Bantam, 1987. (7–12)**
When a young widow realizes she can no longer provide for her six children, she sends them on a train which is carrying orphan children to the Midwest, hoping they will find better lives with new families. One by one, they are adopted by families who are looking for children to love or sometimes to use for cheap labor. The children struggle to forgive their mother for her decision and to accept their new lives.

Applications: Values:
History–Orphan trains of the 1800s   Family relationships,
Sociology–Poverty   Sacrifice, Courage
Psychology–Adoption, Self–esteem

O'Dell, Scott, *The Hawk That Dare Not Hunt by Day.* **Bob Jones Press, 1975. (5–10)**
Told from the perspective of a seaman of the 1500s, this is an account of William Tyndale, the man who put an English translation of the Bible into the hands of the common man. Evading powerful men opposed to his activity, Tyndale smuggles Bibles from clandestine printing presses to those willing to help in his quest.

Applications: Values:
History–The Reformation   Courage, Perseverance

Oke, Janette, *Love Comes Softly.* **Bethany House, 1979. (5–adult)**
Nineteen-year-old Marty is traveling West with her new husband seeking adventure when a disaster leaves her widowed. In the midst of tragedy, an unusual offer of marriage turns Marty's life in a new direction, opening a life of love and fulfillment in spite of the struggles of pioneer life.

Applications:
Histor–Pioneer life
Psychology–Stepfamilies

Values:
Patience, Generosity,
Steadfastness

Orczy, Emmuska (known as Baroness Orczy), *The Scarlet Pimpernel.* **Bantam, 1992. (9–12)**
This historical romance chronicles the activities of a small group of Englishmen who rescue aristocrats from the guillotine during the French Revolution. Their leader, the mysterious Scarlet Pimpernel, is a master of disguise. The action moves from cliff-hanger to cliff-hanger.

Applications:
History–French Revolution
Literature–Adventure, Compare
   to *A Tale of Two Cities*

Values:
Courage, Compassion,
Ingenuity

A Peaceable Kingdom: the Shaker ABECEDARIUS. **Illustrated by Alice and Martin Provensen. Viking Press, 1978. (K–2)**
Little bits of wisdom are added to folk art pictures on the pages of this alphabet book, found originally in a publication of 1882. It contains a mix of both familiar and unfamiliar animals as well as easy and difficult words. Pictures of Shaker life with an afterword by Richard Barsam give insight into this historical time period.

Applications:
Language Arts–Alphabet books
Social Studies–Shakers
Science–Animals

Values:
Thankfulness,
Security

Peart, Jane, *Homeward the Seeking Heart.* **Fleming H. Revell, 1990.** (9–12)
In the spring of 1890, three eight-year-old girls are placed on an orphan train taking homeless children to families in the West, who might adopt them. Toddy is placed in the home of a wealthy widow as companion to her invalid granddaughter. The stories of the two other girls are told in *Quest for Lasting Love* and *Dreams of a Longing Heart.*

Applications: Values:
History–United States, 1850–1900   Faithfulness, Joy,
Psychology–Adoption, Orphans   Perseverance

Pella, Judith, *Frontier Lady/ Stoner's Crossing.* **Bethany House, 1994.** (9–12)
The victim of a physically and emotionally abusive marriage, Deborah Stoner finds herself awaiting execution for the murder of her husband. Though she is rescued once in *Frontier Lady,* the past catches up with her and nineteen years later, in the sequel *Stoner's Crossing,* she goes to trial again. Torn between love for her mother and the incriminating circumstances surrounding her, Deborah's daughter Carolyn must decide where her loyalties belong.

Applications: Values:
History–Frontier life   Self-acceptance,
Psychology–Emotional abuse   Forgiveness

Phillips, Michael and Judith, *My Father's World.* **Bethany House, 1990.** (8–12)
First in a series of eleven books, the text chronicles the pilgrimage of a family of five children who cross the country by covered wagon in search of their errant father. Set in the early 1850s, their adventures accurately depict frontier dangers and lifestyles.

Applications: Values:
History–Frontier life   Courage, Faith,
Psychology–Single parents   Perseverance, Coping
Literature–Journaling

Porter, Gene Stratton, *A Girl of the Limberlost.* Doubleday, 1909. (9–12)
This contains an excellent plot and strongly drawn, realistic characters. There are a number of unexpected twists to reward the reader. It is a story of mystery, deception, bitterness turned to love, death, and a new direction for the heroine's life. For the romance reader, this one far surpasses the sappy fare that is usually found on the paperback rack.

Applications:
History–Turn of the century
Science–Entymology
Psychology–Death of parent,
  Mother/daughter relationships

Values:
Importance of
education, Loyalty,
Integrity, Security

Rawlings, Marjorie Kinan, *The Yearling.* Scribners, 1938, 1985. (8–12) Pulitzer Prize
The most famous of Rawlings's books about Florida backcountry, this title is set in the 1860s when people were wrestling to tame the land. In this story, twelve-year-old Jody's love for a pet deer is pitted against basic issues of hunger and survival.

Applications:
History–Florida
Science–Animal habitat
Literature–Compare to *Shiloh*

Values:
Survival, Love,
Responsibility

Rawls, Wilson, *Where the Red Fern Grows.* Doubleday, 1961. (5–adult)
Billy Coleman wants two coon hounds more than anything else in the world, but he does not have the money to buy them. The experience of working hard to earn the money for his purchase coupled with love and training for his dogs changes his entire life.

Applications:
History–Culture of the Ozarks
Language Arts–Dog stories,
  Recreational reading

Values:
Family relationships,
Work ethic, Love,
Responsibility

Reeder, Carolyn, *Grandpa's Mountain*. Macmillan, 1991. (4–9)

Spending time with her grandparents at their little country store in the mountains of Virginia takes Carrie far from the worries of the Depression. The government's decision to create a national park including the land on which her grandparents live interrupts this peace and changes their lives forever.

Applications:	Values:
History–Great Depression, Appalachia	Family unity, Loyalty, Coping with adversity
Science–Conservation	

Reeder, Carolyn, *Shades of Gray*. Avon/Macmillan, 1989. (5–8) ALA Notable Book

Often overlooked in the aftermath of the Civil War are the children who were orphaned by the tragedy that split our country. Twelve-year-old Will Page, one of those displaced persons, is sent to live on a farm with his uncle, who was a conscientious objector. Will must deal with the hatred he feels for the uncle who refused to fight in the war that took his father.

Applications:	Values:
History–Civil War, Compare to *Jayhawker* and *Across Five Aprils*	Forgiveness

Richardson, Arleta, *In Grandma's Attic*. David C. Cook, 1974. (4–8)

A grandmother's stories of her own growing up provide entertainment, instruction, and understanding for her granddaughter. Arleta Richardson recounts for the reader the treasure of her family's history as it passes from one generation to the next.

Applications:	Values:
History–United States in the late 1800s	Family love
Psychology–Cross-generational relationships	

Rostand, Edmond, *Cyrano de Bergerac.* **Translated by Anthony Burgess, Knopf, 1971. (10–adult)**
Cyrano de Bergerac is filled with the ridiculous and the heroic, overflowing with tears and laughter. Cyrano, a flamboyant hero with a noble romantic spirit, has a large, ugly nose. Though he has learned to defend his honor with poetic flair, he cannot guard his heart against love for the beautiful Roxanne.

Applications:
Literature–French drama,
  Poetry
History–France in the 1800s,
  Thirty Years' War

Values:
Self-sacrifice,
Humor, Love

Scott, Sir Walter, *Ivanhoe.* **Dodd, Mead, 1820, 1979. (9–12)**
The setting for Scott's lengthy book is England after the Norman Conquest. In spite of its difficult language, this is a valuable portrayal of the drama, romance, chivalry, and political intrigue that lay behind the pageantry of the Middle Ages.

Applications:
History–Middle Ages,
  Prejudice against Jews
Literature–Advanced readers

Values:
Sacrifice, Courage,
Chivalry

Serraillier, Ian, *Escape from Warsaw.* **Scholastic, 1970. (9–12)**
Pursued by Nazi secret police, who have arrested their mother, the Balicki children escape Warsaw, making their way across war-ravaged Europe through Czechoslovakia, Germany, and Austria. Their ultimate goal is Switzerland, where they believe their father will be waiting for them. This story of three young refugees and the harrowing trip they endure is based on actual events.

Applications:
History–World War II, Europe
Psychology–Survival

Values:
Cooperation, Courage,
Family unity,
Perseverance

Sorensen, Virginia, *Miracles on Maple Hill*. Illustrated by Beth and Joe Krush. Scholastic, 1956. (5–10) Newbery Medal
Mother is worried and Daddy is tired all the time when Marty's family moves from the city to the small farmhouse on Maple Hill. As spring begins to touch the woods and fields around them, however, one miracle after another begins to unfold, bringing healing and hope for a new future.

Applications:	Values:
Geography–Pennsylvania	Family unity,
Science–Woods, Maple syrup production	Unselfishness, Nature appreciation

Speare, Elizabeth George, *The Bronze Bow*. Houghton Mifflin, 1961. (7–12) Newbery Medal
Daniel Bar Jamin, a zealot who hates the Romans who are responsible for the death of his parents, joins a band of outlaws believing that they will be successful in destroying the Romans. Daniel lives a life filled with bitterness and the desire for revenge, until he meets a teacher whom people call Jesus.

Applications:	Values:
History–Roman Empire, Jewish family life	Courage, Friendship, Ethnic acceptance,
Literature–Dramatization	Healing

Speare, Elizabeth George, *The Sign of the Beaver*. Houghton Mifflin, 1983. (5–8)
Left in the Maine wilderness to protect the new cabin while his father returns for the rest of the family, Matt loses his gun to a thief and much of his store of food to a marauding bear. Through the help of Attean, grandson of an Indian chief, he learns the skills necessary to survive.

Applications:	Values:
Social Studies–Frontier life	Courage, Cooperation
Pioneer/Indian relationships	Resourcefulness,

Shemin, Margaretha, *The Little Riders.* Beech Tree Books, 1988. (5–8)

Johanna loves the metal figures on horseback who ride out from behind little doors on the clock of the old church tower in their Dutch village. When occupying German forces threaten to melt these riders down to use the metal, Johanna risks her life to help her grandfather save them.

Applications: Values:
History–World War II, Holland   Courage, Loyalty
Psychology–Cross–generational
  relationships

Steele, William O., *The Far Frontier.* Harcourt Brace, 1959. (3–8)

When Asa Twistletree comes to study the natural habitat of the western frontier region, the settlers think he is a fool. He does not even know how to hunt or start a fire. Toby Bledsoe feels betrayed when he is bound out to work with the man, but he finds that courage and integrity come in many forms.

Applications: Values:
Social Studies–Frontier life,   Ingenuity, Courage,
  Pioneer/Indian relationships   Sacrifice
Science–Conservation

Stevenson, Robert Louis, *Kidnapped.* Grosset and Dunlap, 1886, 1948. (9–12)

In an attempt to cheat him of his inheritance, David Balfour's uncle arranges to have him kidnapped and taken to sea. While at sea, David meet Alan Breck, a fleeing Jacobite leader. Together the comrades endure sea battles, perilous chases across Scotland, and a mysterious murder.

Applications: Values:
History–Scotland, Research   Loyalty, Friendship,
  family history   Survival
Literature–Mystery

Thoene, Bodie, *In My Father's House.* Bethany House, 1992 (9–12)

Soldiers returning from the battlefields of World War I face another kind of battle at home. As the forces of racial, religious, and cultural intolerance threaten to pull their families apart, love and friendship work to hold them together.

Applications:
History–World War I, Racial
  relations
Literature–Introduction to the
  Shiloh series

Values:
Courage, Friendship,
Family love, Faith

Thoene, Bodie and Brock, *The Twilight of Courage.* Thomas Nelson, 1994. (9–adult)

As war clouds gather over Europe, the Thoenes weave together the lives of American journalists and pilots, Polish refugees, French, German, and English soldiers and orphaned children, in suspenseful and heart-rending events. This book lays the groundwork for events that continue in two series detailing the repercussions of World War II, entitled *The Zion Chronicles* and *The Zion Covenant.*

Applications:
History–World War II, Cultural
  conflict
Literature–Survival stories

Values:
Courage, Compassion,
Loyalty

Tripp, Valerie, *Molly's Christmas.* Pleasant Company, 1986. (3–8)

With their father serving in the armed forces in an English hospital and their grandparents unable to make the trip for Christmas, the McIntires are facing a lonely holiday. Mr. McIntire, however, finds a way to make Christmas special for his family, even from afar.

Applications:
Social Studies–World War II,
Language Arts–Use with other
  stories in the *American Girl* series

Values:
Family love

Wells, Rosemary, *Waiting for the Evening Star*. Illustrated by Susan Jeffers. Dial Books, 1994. (K–4)
Exquisite paintings illustrate this nostalgic look at New England farm life at the turn of the century. Together, the author and illustrator celebrate an era when time seemed to move more slowly, when families worked and played together, and neighbor helped neighbor, swapping one skill for another. This is a timeless book, worthy of a permanent place in any collection.

Applications:
Social Studies–United States in the 1800s, New England, Farm life

Values:
Cooperation, Family unity, Community life

Wilder, Laura Ingalls, *Little House on the Prairie*. Illustrated by Garth Williams. Harper & Row, 1935. (3–6)
This story of a pioneer family is loved as a classic by children, though it never won an award. It contains the joys and heartaches that were common in early frontier America.

Applications:
Social Studies–Pioneer life, Wisconsin
Language Arts–Reading aloud, Compare to *The Courage of Sarah Noble*

Values:
Family unity, Work ethic, Cooperation

Wood, Audrey, *King Bidgood's in the Bathtub*. Illustrated by Don Wood. Harcourt, Brace, Jovanovich, 1985. (K–3)
King Bidgood is enjoying himself so much in the bathtub that he will not come out. After many nobles try unsuccessfully to coax him out, the resourceful page succeeds.

Applications:
Language Arts–Write about what life as King would be like
Health–Cleanliness

Values:
Humor, Creativity

CHAPTER SIX
CONTEMPORARY FICTION

Being an adolescent has never been easy. History records the sibling rivalry of Cain and Abel, the near-sacrifice of Isaac by his father, Abraham, and the chastening words of the mother of twelve-year-old Jesus when she asks, "Where were you? Didn't you know that we would be worried?" Although these are all examples penned thousands of years ago, similar trials exist today for the adolescent. Young adults are still jealous of their brothers or sisters, still have fears about situations over which they have no control, and still cause parents to lose sleep.

Often, writers of contemporary fiction attempt to aid their readers in making a smoother, less lonely transition from childhood to adulthood by writing about situations that shadow the lives of young people. Whether the crisis is dealing with the suicide of a friend, as in *Singin' Somebody Else's Song* (Christian), or surviving divorce, as in *The Solomon System* (Naylor), the way may be made easier if one can read about the struggles and final success of another who has walked the same road and come through a similar trial victoriously. Many books available on contemporary shelves are awash with submission to peer pressure, contain objectionable language and often present compromising solutions to problems that appeal to the baser nature of the reading teen. Others tend to make all adults look foolish, shallow, or hopelessly closed-minded. We have tried to present a balanced view of these complex problems facing young people by presenting titles that give the adolescent protagonist the freedom to make adult decisions without negating the intelligence and compassion of a significant adult, thus establishing a precious bridge across the chasm of age.

All is not somber and problem-filled, however. The humor of Betsy Byars as she focuses on such varied topics as first love, in *The Burning Questions of Bingo Brown,* and blended families-to-be, in *The Animal, The Vegetable and John D. Jones,* lightens the mood while taking an honest look at changes which take place in the lives of many adolescents. Gordon Korman provides unadulterated laughter in *This Can't Be Happening at MacDonald Hall,* as he introduces us to plots hatched by the residents of a boys' school in Canada.

For the elementary reader, as well as the adolescent who enjoys animal stories, we suggest the classic tales of Walter Farley, represented here by *The Black Stallion,* or Jim Kjelgaard's *Big Red.* For the sports fan, Matt Christopher's combination of athletics and mystery is found between the covers of *Tackle Without a Team.* Of course, we have included a representative sampling of Beverly Cleary's ever-popular stories of a boy and his dog, *Henry and Ribsy,* as well as other beloved Cleary books.

Children who are dealing with their own physical handicaps or the physical or mental disabilities of siblings or other adults living in their homes face a special set of challenges. To meet those needs, we have selected books that depict such environments with realism, candor, and compassion. Jean Little writes about a child's struggles with cerebral palsy in *Mine for Keeps.* June Rae Wood addresses problems that arise when families disagree about what is best for an adult with Down's Syndrome in *The Man Who Loved*

Clowns. Both positive and negative effects upon siblings of children with multiple handicaps are explored in *Father's Arcane Daughter* by E. L. Konigsburg. Making selections from the almost overwhelming number of contemporary fiction books available today has been a difficult task, and we do not consider our selections by any means to be all-inclusive. Even now, we are planning what to add in the next edition. However, we feel that with limited space, we have chosen those that meet our criteria and provide a pleasing variety. Not all books in this section may be termed classic literature, but we have chosen those that children and young adults will enjoy, that will fill a particular need in their lives, and certainly those that end with hope. Someone has defined young adult literature as those books which young people choose to read, not those which are required. We have attempted to recommend those that the child or young adult would choose to read, not once, but several times.

Most of the works we have cited are for elementary and secondary age readers. Comparable books for the young reader are found in the chapter focusing on picture books. Likewise, those selections dealing with people of color are for the most part discussed in the chapter emphasizing multicultural friendships, families, or main characters. We made that choice because we felt that such books would be easier to locate if grouped together in a way that celebrated diversity, rather than having them swallowed up under the conglomerate heading of Contemporary Fiction.

Finally, we wish to define the terms that form the framework of this chapter. The term "contemporary" is used here to refer to any story that takes place within the time period that we would think of as a generation. In this chapter, all our stories are set within the last forty years, except for three classic animal stories. Since dogs and horses do not change very much over a decade, a dog in 1945 would be about the same as a dog in 1955.

Life for children in the nineties may mean a traditional family with one mother, one father, and one house. More often, however, modern children will be faced with multiple changes, and perhaps multiple or single parents. Today's children, instead of visiting with grandparents every Sunday or even every summer, may hardly know any relatives other than those with whom they live. Because of parental job loss, change, or promotion, the children in the last decade of the twentieth century may live in many states and more than one foreign country in the eighteen or more years that they live with their parents. The books we have chosen are those which provide examples of homes in which children feel secure, whether living with one or two parents, with grandparents, in one town or many. We have attempted to share messages of security with children who are growing up in a very insecure world, and yet give them characters who are engaged in struggles like their own. It is our hope that stronger bonds will be forged in their relationships, and that their lives may be greatly enriched through reading these books.

Arthur, Randall, *Wisdom Hunter.* Questar Publishing, 1991. (9–12)
When Jason Faircloth, a strict, domineering pastor, loses all that matters in life as a result of his unyielding spirit, he leaves the ministry and goes in search of wisdom. What he discovers is international intrigue and danger. Ultimately, he finds peace and a place of service. A page turner, this is not a comfortable book to read–but is one the reader will not forget.

Applications:	Values:
Psychology–Parents and children injured by legalism	Healing, Faith
Language Arts–Mystery and detective stories	

Avi, *Shadrach's Crossing.* Pantheon Books, 1983. (5–12)
Shad Faherty and his family live in poverty on an island in the post-depression years. As a result of Prohibition, smugglers are using their tiny island as a transportation route for illegal alcoholic beverages. The powerful criminals control the population of the island through fear. Although he is only twelve, Shad determines to brave all odds to stop the smugglers.

Applications:	Values:
Social Studies–Prohibition era	Courage, Ingenuity,
Language Arts–Creative writing	Morality
Psychology–Problem solving	

Avi, *S.O.R. Losers.* Bradbury Press, 1984. (5–9)
This is a tongue-in-cheek story of a team of academically bright but athletically dull seventh-grade boys who are required to play soccer as their one team sport. It is especially humorous as told in the first person voice by the reluctant goalie.

Applications:	Values:
Language Arts–Recreational reading for the unathletic, Reluctant readers, Role playing	Self-acceptance, Humor, Team work

Benjamin, Carol Lea, *Nobody's Baby Now.* **Macmillan, 1984. (9–12)**
This fast-paced, easy-to-read story operates on the crisis level of three generations, but the reader sees all three from the first-person view of overweight, bespectacled Olivia Singer, aged fifteen. Liv, as her friends call her, has a crush on Brian, who really sees her as "just one of the guys." The crisis of Liv's crush on Brian fades into the background when grandmother, who is apparently in a catatonic state, is moved into the apartment until a good nursing home can be found. Liv and her parents experience the helpless pain of seeing their loved one in this condition. Through love and determination, Liv eventually gains a revealing response from her grandmother. Through jogging and dieting, she also obtains a positive response from Brian.

Applications: Values:
Health–Nutrition and exercise   Self–reliance, Love,
Psychology–Cross-generational   Decision-making,
  relationships, Illness of   Unselfishness
  loved one
Literature–Recreational reading

Bridgers, Sue Ellen, *Notes for Another Life.* **Bantam Books, 1981. (9–12)**
Kevin and Wren, like many children who live in nontraditional family stiuations, fantasize about the time when their mother can fit them into her life along with her career and their father will be emotionally stable enough to be a real dad. Living with loving grandparents who are loyal to their parents and try to give the children a stable home does not totally fill the void. However, the demands of her music give structure to Wren's life and even soothe Kevin as both youngsters teeter on the brink of becoming adults.

Applications: Values:
Psychology–Mentally ill parents,   Family unity,
  Cross-generational relationships,   Individuality
  Coming of age, Music as
  therapy

Bunting, Eve, *Fly away Home.* **Illustrated by Ronald Himler. Clarion Books, 1991. (1–4)**
A young boy and his father joining other homeless people who live at the airport follow one rule very closely: Do not do anything to be noticed. One day as the young boy is carrying luggage to make extra money while his father is at work, he is encouraged to see a bird that has been trapped in the terminal fly out the door to freedom. With great sensitivity, Bunting and Himler present a difficult subject from a child's-eye view.

Applications: Values:
Social Studies–Homelessness   Family unity, Ingenuity,
Psychology–Survival   Cooperation
Language Arts–Reading aloud

Bunting, Eve, *Such Nice Kids.* **Clarion Books, 1990, (9–12)**
Jason's parents are out of town and he is left at home alone. When Pidge, Jason's friend, needs a car for a special date, a third friend, Meeker, convinces Jason that he should lend Pidge his mother's car. One deception leads to another until there is irreversible tragedy.

Applications: Values:
Literature–Reluctant readers   Honesty, Responsibility
Psychology–Peer pressure

Byars, Betsy, *The Animal, The Vegetable and John D. Jones.* **Delacorte Press, 1982. (5–8)**
Two single parents wish to merge families by marriage and as a "trial run" choose to take a vacation together. The three junior-high-aged children do not try to get along together until a near-tragedy focuses on the things that are really important in life. Strong characterization makes this a novel to remember.

Applications: Values:
Psychology–Single parenting   Family unity,
Language Arts–Journaling,   Cooperation,
  Predicting, Role playing   Communication

Byars, Betsy, *The Burning Questions of Bingo Brown.*
Viking Kestrel, 1988. (5–8)
Experiencing all the trauma of first love, or rather loves–since our
hero is in love with three other preteens at the same time–Bingo
Brown gives the reader personal glimpses into those earth-
shattering days of eighth grade. Byars has the reader laughing
aloud at Bingo's escapades yet sensing that more serious issues are
at stake. Hyperbole in the title is an excellent choice, as the reader
will discover as this multileveled plot unfolds.

Applications:	Values:
Psychology–Dealing with suicide	Friendship, Loyalty,
Art–Design a tee shirt	Compassion

Byars, Betsy, *Cracker Jackson.* **Viking Kestrel, 1985.**
(5–8)
When Jackson Hunter discovers that his beloved babysitter is being
abused by her husband, he tries to help. When nothing he does as
a child seems to work, he decides to play the adult role–with the
help of his best friend, Goat. The results will bring tears of
tenderness as well as tears of laughter to the eyes of most readers
as once again Byars manages to infuse humor into tragedy.

Applications:	Values:
Social Studies–Research laws	Decision making,
governing abuse and	Loyalty, Friendship
facilities for battered women	
Language Arts–Creative writing	

Byars, Betsy, *The Summer of the Swans.* **Viking Penguin,**
1970. (5–9) Newbery Award
For Sara Godfrey the precarious adolescent time is made more
difficult by an absentee father and no mother. The only safe haven
is her mentally handicapped brother, Charlie. When Charlie dis-
appears, Sara learns important lessons about herself, her family and
a neighbor boy whom she hates.

Applications:	Values:
Psychology–Handicapped siblings,	Family unity,
Single parenting	Friendship

Caudill, Rebecca, *Did You Carry the Flag Today Charley?* Illustrated by Nancy Grossman. Holt, Rinehart and Winston, 1966. (K–4)
Charley, a five-year-old living in the Kentucky mountains, is having his first taste of the outside world through an introductory summer school session. All of the wonders of a classroom, added to Charley's boundless curiosity, makes it almost impossible for him to behave.

Applications:
Language Arts–Predicting
Psychology–Active children
Social Studies–Kentucky

Values:
Perseverance, Humor,
Family unity

Christian, Mary B., *Growin' Pains.* Macmillan, 1985. (9–12)
Set in Clemmons, Texas, this story of growing up poor will warm the heart. Ginny Ruth, deserted by her father and not understood by her mother, copes with life by writing poetry. Through this creative expression, she establishes a relationship with an older man who is hampered by a frustrating handicap. Their friendship enables the young poet to rise above her "growin' pains."

Applications:
Health–Coping with handicaps
Psychology–Single parenting

Values:
Finding one's gift,
Cross-generational
friendships

Christian, Mary B., *Singin' Somebody Else's Song.* Macmillan, 1988. (9–12)
Propelled by guilt following the suicide of his best friend, seventeen-year-old Gideon arrives in Nashville to "make it" in the country music field. Battered by a barrage of rejections, he turns to an attractive young waitress for encouragement. Through difficult decisions, Gideon discovers what he really wants and who he is.

Applications:
Literature–Compare to *Come Sing, Jimmy Jo*
Psychology–Dealing with suicide

Values:
Self-awareness, Family
unity, Friendship

Christopher, Matt, *Tackle Without a Team*. Illustrated by Margaret Sanfilippo. Little Brown, 1989. (5–9)
This small volume includes fast-paced dialogue, with enough huddle and locker room jargon to arrest the attention of the active football enthusiast, and the mystery of a whodunit. After being dismissed from the team because marijuana is found in his duffel bag, Scott Kramer sets out to find who placed it there, and to clear his name.

Applications:	Values:
Literature–Reluctant readers	Perseverance,
Physical Education–Sports	Setting goals

Cleary, Beverly, *Dear Mr. Henshaw*. Illustrated by Paul O. Zelinsky, Dell, 1983. (5–8) Newbery Award
This small yet significant book covers a critical time period from second through sixth grade in the life of Leigh Botts. During these years, Leigh corresponds with his favorite author, Mr. Henshaw, who encourages his young fan to keep a journal. This practice becomes a form of therapy at a time in Leigh's life when he most needs it.

Applications:	Values:
Language Arts–Journaling,	Self-reliance, Coping,
Classroom reading	Finding one's gift,
Psychology–Parental separation,	Cross-generational
New child in school	friendship

Cleary, Beverly, *Henry and Ribsy*. Morrow, 1954. (5–8)
Henry Huggins is the kind of red-blooded American boy that humorous things just happen to, especially since he got Ribsy, his nondescript mutt of a dog. Henry and Ribsy are both totally believable, yet find themselves in unbelievably amusing situations. This book will appeal to readers across age and gender lines.

Applications:	Values:
Language Arts–Reading aloud,	Friendship, Humor,
Dramatization	Responsibility

Clearly, Beverly, *Strider*. Illustrated by Paul O. Zelinsky. William Morrow, 1991. (5–9)

This sequel to the very popular *Dear Mr. Henshaw* does not disappoint the reader. As Leigh has matured, he has found a friend in whose home he experiences large family atmosphere. Into this blissful setting comes a dog–loved by both boys. Assorted crises make this another realistic Cleary masterpiece, leaving the reader with a feeling of satisfaction and a hope there might be a *Strider II*.

Applications:

Values:

Language Arts–Compare to *Dear Mr. Henshaw,* Journaling

Psychology–Joint custody

Friendship, Family unity, Maturity, Love of animals

Creech, Sharon, *Walk Two Moons*. HarperCollins, 1994. (5–12) Newbery Award

Salamanca Tree and her father have been deserted by her mother. To help her adjust, Sal's grandparents take her to the location where her mother was last seen. En route, Sal passes the time by telling of a friend whose mother had to deal with deep dark secrets as well. Not a traditional family story, this lesson in forgiveness, acceptance, and strong family ties will meet needs of many young adults.

Applications:

Values:

History–Native Americans

Psychology–Desertion, Single parenting, Cross-generational relationships

Acceptance, Love, Family unity

Cunningham, Julia, *The Silent Voice*. Dell, 1981. (5–12)

Astair is a plucky girl who leads a group of waifs trying to survive on the streets of Paris. The group saves the life of Auguste, a mute boy who has aspirations of becoming a mime. Auguste overcomes strong prejudice and jealousy in his struggle to achieve his dream.

Applications:

Values:

History–Paris

Psychology–Survival, Handicaps

Compassion, Finding one's gift

Farley, Walter, *The Black Stallion.* **Random, 1941. (5–9)**
Shipwreck, survival, the love of a boy for a horse, and finally the
fame and success of winning a coveted prize are the ingredients of
this adventure novel that has become a classic. This is the first in
the series that has become popular with middle school boys and
girls.

Applications:	Values:
Literature–Reluctant readers,	Responsibility,
Recreational reading	Perseverance,
Science–Horses, Pet care	Setting a goal

Farley, Walter, *The Great Dane Thor.* **Illustrated by
Joseph Cellini. Random, 1966. (5–12)**
Although Farley writes a good dog story, this book is more
importantly about a father and son who have difficulty com-
municating. Thor, the great Dane, and the training he is given to
respect wildlife, becomes the catalyst of understanding within the
family.

Applications:	Values:
Literature–Compare dog stories	Communication,
Psychology–Parent/child	Respect for all forms
relationships	of life
History–Wildlife in New England	

Fox, Paula, *One-Eyed Cat.* **Dell, 1984. (5–12) Newbery
Honor**
Ned is the only child of a minister and a bedridden mother. His life
is rather routine and predictable, presided over by the pessimistic
housekeeper, Mrs. Scallop, until the visit from world traveler Uncle
Hilary. This adventurous bachelor brings him a rifle but Ned's
father forbids him to use it. Ned disobeys, and accidently wounds,
or believes that he wounds, a cat. He later confesses and maturity
comes with the lessons learned.

Applications:	Values:
Literature–Write other solutions	Cross-generational
Psychology–Guilt, Living with	friendships, Trust,
handicapped parent	Obedience

George, Jean Craighead, *My Side of The Mountain.*
Dutton, 1959. (5–9) Newbery Honor
When summer in the city with his large family becomes too much
for teenager Sam Gribley, he returns to the mountain from which
his ancestors came. With his parents' blessing, he lives alone for
a year, learning to live off the land and yet remain in harmony with
his natural surroundings. Author George is recognized as a
naturalist, and her details of survival are accurate as well as
interesting and appealing to the outdoor enthusiast. A sequel to
this work, entitled *The Other Side of The Mountain,* is also
available.

Applications: Values:
Science–Ecology   Respect for nature
Practical Arts–Survival skills in
   cooking and home building
Literature–Recreational reading
Psychology–Developing autonomy,
   Survival

Giff, Patricia Reilly, *The Beast in Ms. Rooney's Room.*
Illustrated by Blance Sims, Dell, 1984. (K–4)
In her series The Kids of Polk Street School, Patricia Reilly Giff
has done teachers, students, and parents a great favor. She has
written some great short stories in individual book format, with
easy-to-read vocabulary and plots that adults and children alike will
enjoy. In the above mentioned work, Richard Best (otherwise
known as "the Beast") suffers through having his best friend move
away, and discovers that he has to go to summer school to improve
his reading. The book, while realistic, is not depressing and teaches
young readers to face difficulty with a sense of humor and a belief
that they can cope.

Applications: Values:
Language Arts–Easy reading,   Coping with problems,
   Reading aloud   Humor
Psychology–Role playing problems,
   Friendship

Hall, Barbara, *Dixie Storms.* Harcourt, Brace, Jovanovich, 1990. (9–12)
As the dry ground cracks from lack of rain, so the world of Dutch Peyton seems to deteriorate. Creditors assess the farm as Dutch assesses her city cousin Norma, who has come to spend her summer in the country. Just when all appears to be lost and family relationships are most precarious, the healing rains fall, and Dutch discovers a relationship which allows her world to come securely together.

Applications:	Values:
Literature–Recreational reading	Family unity, Coming
Social Studies–South	of age, Cross-generational relationships
Psychology–Parental separation	ational relationships

Henry, Marguerite, *King of the Wind.* Rand McNally, 1948, 1984. (5–8) Newbery Award
Beginning with the last glorious race of Man O'War, Henry uses flashback to trace the heroic ancestry of the world-famous horse. Even for the reader who does not favor horse stories, this well-documented story is hard to put down.

Applications:	Values:
Social Studies–Morocco	Dedication, Loyalty,
Science–Caring for horses	Courage
Literature–Compare horse stories	

Henry, Marguerite, *Misty of Chicoteague.* Illustrated by Wesley Dennis. Rand McNally, 1948. (3–8) Newbery Honor
Pony penning, the annual drive of wild horses from their natural habitat to waiting horse lovers, provides the backdrop for this near-classic story. Caught by caring children, Misty proves to be a most unusual pony developing almost human characteristics. Illustrations include photographs of this famous partnership of boy, girl, and horse.

Applications:	Values:
Social Studies–Virginia	Respect for animals,
Science–Coastal wildlife,	Responsibility,
Pet care, Horses	Cooperation

Kjelgaard, Jim, *Big Red*. Illustrated by Bob Kuhn. Holiday House, 1945. (5–9)
Trapping, hunting, and whatever hard work it takes to wrest survival from timberland is the life of seventeen-year-old Danny Pickett and his dad. However, such a spare existence does not prevent the realization of Danny's dream of caring for a beautiful Irish setter show dog. Danny and Big Red share a love of adventure and each other that the reader will long remember. This author is acclaimed as one who builds excellent stories around animal/human relationships. *Big Red* was chosen as a representative sample of his work.

Applications:	Values:
Literature–Introduction to author	Responsibility, Courage,
Science–Research wilderness life,	Perseverance
Pet care	
Psychology–Single parenting	

Konigsburg, E. L., *Father's Arcane Daughter*. Dell, 1976. (5–12)
Konigsburg has packed a powerful story of mystery, money, and a physically challenged child into this compact book. The secure, routine, and boring lives of affluent Winston and Heidi Carmichael are changed forever when Caroline arrives unannounced at their home. The beautiful young woman claims to be their half-sister who had been kidnapped and reportedly killed in the rescue attempt more than a decade ago. Finally accepted by the father, never by the stepmother, Caroline undertakes to assist the disabled Heidi to reach her full potential, and to free Winston from the undue responsibility that has fallen upon him.

Applications:	Values:
Literature–Reading aloud,	Perseverance, Love
Making predictions	
Psychology–Family dealing with	
handicapped child, Sibling	
relationships	

Korman, Gordon, *This Can't Be Happening At Mac-Donald Hall.* **Scholastic, 1978.** **(5–9)**
Set in a boys' academy in Canada, this little book that Korman wrote while in the seventh grade should be required reading for every child during his elementary school years. Bruno and Boots will keep even the most reluctant reader entertained. Korman has the knack for making the most unusual prank seem possible, even probable. What an inspiration for an aspiring young writer!

Applications: Values:
Psychology–Laughter as medicine   Humor, Friendship
Social Studies–Canada
Language Arts–Encouraging young
  authors, Reluctant readers

L'Engle, Madeleine, *The Arm of the Starfish.* **American Book, 1965.** **(5–12)**
Meg Murry and Calvin O'Keefe from L'Engle's Time Trilogy share this adventure story set in Portugal. Dr. O'Keefe has discovered how regeneration may be used in human healing, but subversive and greedy forces are attempting to steal and market his discovery for their own profit.

Applications: Values:
Literature–Prediction   Perseverance, Courage,
History–Portugal   Family unity
Science–Uses of research

L'Engle, Madeleine, *Meet the Austins.* **Dell, 1960.** **(5–12)**
When tragedy strikes a friend of the family, Dr. and Mrs. Austin choose to help and find themselves with a small, spoiled, bitter orphan girl to care for. Each member of the family learns valuable lessons from their time together, including Maggy, the grieving child.

Applications: Values:
Literature–Compare to *Shades of*   Coping with grief,
  Gray   Family unity, Sharing
Psychology–Loss of parent

Levene, Nancy, *Crocodile Meatloaf.* **Chariot, 1993. (K–4)**
Alex befriends Rachel, a newcomer to her sixth-grade class. With this relationship comes the role of protection from cruel teasing by the class bully because Rachel is deaf.

Applications:
Language Arts–Reading aloud
Health–Handicaps
Psychology–Siblings of handicapped
Science–Deafness

Values:
Friendship, Courage

Little, Jean, *Mine for Keeps.* **Little, Brown, 1962. (5–9)**
After learning special skills that will help her cope with life as a survivor of cerebral palsy, Sally is returning home and facing the adjustments of living with her family. The responses of her family and friends, as well as Sally's adjustment to a more "normal" environment, make this an unforgettable story.

Applications:
Health–Dealing with handicaps
Psychology–Coping with cerebral
  palsy

Values:
Survival, Compassion,
Self-acceptance,
Family unity

Lowry, Lois, *Rabble Starkey.* **Houghton Mifflin, 1987. (5–12)**
Rabble and her mother live in a garage apartment on the property of the wealthy Bigelow family. Mrs. Bigelow is ill, and Rabble's mom is both housekeeper and nanny for the daughter, Veronica. As Rabble and Veronica become friends, the confidence and contagious love of life shared by Rabble and her mother spills over to Veronica, and to her hurting father. A Boston Globe–Horn Book Award winner, this book demonstrates unselfish love in a way the reader will not forget.

Applications:
Literature–Compare with *Notes*
  for Another Life or *Strider*
Psychology–Single parenting,
  Mental illness

Values:
Integrity, Love,
Friendship across
social status lines

Lyon, George Ella, *Borrowed Children.* **Franklin Watts, 1988. (4–10)**
When her mother nearly dies in childbirth, Amanda must assume responsibility for the baby and her brother and sister as well as the house. Carrying her burdens with admirable courage, she is still real enough to show discouragement. Lyon sprinkles in ample humor to prevent the story from becoming depressing and brings Amanda through a worthwhile journey of self-discovery.

Applications:	Values:
History–Kentucky	Responsibility,
Psychology–Siblings, Family	Family unity
heritage, Self-acceptance	

MacLachlan, Patricia, *The Facts and Fiction of Minna Pratt.* **Harper & Row, 1988. (5–8)**
At chamber music lessons, Minna, whose mother writes children's books and doesn't clean house very often, meets Lucas Ellerby, whose mother is so fastidious that she will not allow her son to own a pet. This is a memorable story of first love and family acceptance.

Applications:	Values:
Literature–Recreational reading	Love, Family unity,
Music–Chamber instruments	Creativity
Psychology–Self-acceptance,	
Family acceptance, Gifted child	

MacLachlan, Patricia, *Journey.* **Delacorte Press, 1991. (5–8)**
MacLachlan chronicles the journey of a small boy of the same name through the feelings of desertion, anger, bitterness, and other responses that arise in the wake of a mother's choice to leave her children. Healing comes through facing reality with the aid of loving grandparents, and the unlikely assistance of a camera and a cat.

Applications:	Values:
Language Arts–Journaling	Family unity, Love,
Art–Photography	Cross-generational
Psychology–Desertion	relationships, Love

Mazer, Norma Fox, *After the Rain.* **Avon, 1987. (9–12)**
Fifteen-year-old Rachel has a unique problem. Her parents think
she can do no wrong. They spoil and smother her with attention
and affection. Her escape comes through her cranky old grandfather, who apparently thinks no one is right about anything. Quite
by accident, Rachel becomes responsible for her grandfather's
welfare. The two develop a special relationship which both desperately need.

Applications: Values:
Literature–Journaling, Letter   Love, Respect
  writing
Health–Aging
History–Research family origins

McDaniel, Lurlene, *Now I Lay Me Down to Sleep.*
Bantam, 1991. (9–12)
A cancer support group meeting provides the opportunity for
fifteen-year-old Carrie Blake to meet Keith, a young man she comes
to value greatly. Both must deal with the specter of the possible
return of cancer while attempting to lead normal lives. Never
morbid, yet realistic, this story meets head-on the problems faced by
young people with terminal illness.

Applications: Values:
Psychology–Terminal illness   Courage, Friendship,
Health–Coping with illness   Family unity

McDaniel, Lurlene, *Sixteen and Dying.* **Bantam, 1992.
(9–12)**
Anne Wingate has been granted one last wish by a mysterious
benefactor shortly after being diagnosed HIV-positive. Her fatal
disease is the result of a contaminated transfusion received prior to
1985. In this quickly read novel, McDaniel reveals the facts and
feelings of a teenager trapped by the AIDS virus. The wide-open
spaces of a dude ranch frame most of the setting for this brave
young woman's battle.

Applications: Values:
Literature–Individual reading   Courage
Psychology–Terminal illness

**Myers, Walter Dean, *Somewhere in the Darkness.*
Scholastic, 1992. (5–12) Caldecott Honor**
This is the story of a unique parent-child relationship, forged by a
father who escapes from jail. Crab is determined that his son will
know him and have something to remember that they did together
before he dies.

Applications: Values:
Literature–Creative writing,   Compassion, Father/
  Compare with single-parent stories   son relationships,
Psychology–Single parenting   Forgiveness

**Naylor, Phyllis Reynolds, *Shiloh.* Atheneum, 1991. (3–8)
Newbery Medal**
When eleven-year-old Marty is adopted by a stray dog, he faces
opposition from two directions. Shiloh, the name Marty gives to
the little beagle, already has an owner, and there is no money in the
family funds to feed a pet. Torn between his clandestine love for the
abused dog and family responsibility, Marty negotiates a creative
solution that leaves the reader fulfilled and smiling.

Applications: Values:
Language Arts–Group reading   Ingenuity, Integrity,
Psychology–Abuse   Honesty, Compassion
Science–Pet care, Research dogs

**Naylor, Phyllis Reynolds, *The Solomon System.* Athe-
neum, 1985. (9–12)**
Ted and Nory Solomon are brothers who have been so close and
worked so well together that a neighbor coined the term "Solomon
System" to describe them. As Nory reaches nineteen, and Ed
thirteen, their relationship weakens and the boys become aware of
increasing tension between their parents, which eventually results
in separation. Grandma Rose proves to be their mainstay
throughout the crisis.

Applications: Values:
Psychology–Sibling relationships   Coping, Love, Finding
  Coming of age, Separation   one's own identity

Oke, Janette, *Pordy's Prickly Problem.* Bethel, 1993. (K–4)
Pordy Porcupine is afraid to try anything new–from climbing trees to making new friends.   As Pordy matures, her mother demonstrates patience and encouragement which helps Pordy overcome her fears and lack of self-confidence.   A well-written animal story that has significance for every child beset by shyness.

Applications: Values:
Language Arts–Easy reading   Courage, Maturity,
Psychology–Single parenting,   Family unity
   Shyness

Parish, Peggy, *Merry Christmas Amelia Bedelia.* William Morrow, 1986. (K–4)
Amelia Bedelia is left to prepare for Christmas Eve with the customary list from Mrs. Rogers.   As usual, she gets her instructions confused when she makes a date cake, trims the tree and prepares a Christmas carol surprise.

Applications: Values:
Language Arts–Reading aloud,   Humor
   Figurative language

Paterson, Katherine, *Bridge to Terabithia.* Crowell, 1977. (5–9) Newbery Award
Being a boy in fifth grade who aspires to be an artist rather isolates Jesse Aarons from other significant males in his life.   Being new in a rural school, and being a very fast runner, somewhat sets Leslie apart from most other females.   Coming together as friends and creating an imaginary land in which both can be themselves cements the relationship between the two outsiders.   In Terabithia, they escape feelings of rejection and affirm their individuality, building inner strength so that when tragedy strikes, healing arises from hurt.

Applications: Values:
Language Arts–Reading aloud,   Friendship, Family
Discussing psychological dynamics   unity, Individuality
Psychology–Grieving, Self-esteem

Paterson, Katherine, *Come Sing, Jimmy Jo*. Lodestar Books, 1985. (5–9)
Eleven-year-old James Johnson is rapidly becoming a reluctant star rising in the country music sky, when what he really wishes to do is be back in the hills with his beloved grandmother. This coming-of-age story pays great tribute to a memorable cross-generational relationship.

Applications:
Language Arts–Compare to
  Trouble River
Psychology–Loneliness, Parental
  strife, Homesickness

Values:
Cross-generational
relationships, Love,
Finding one's talent,
Cross-cultural
friendship

Patterson, Nancy, *The Christmas Cup*. Illustrated by Leslie Bowman. Orchard Books, 1989 (3–8)
When Ann Megan McCallie spends her lemonade stand money on an old, dented and rusty milkshake cup her wise grandmother helps her turn it into a thing of beauty and blessing. This warm-hearted story will be enjoyed not only at Christmas but throughout the year.

Applications:
Language Arts–Creative writing
  about other uses for the cup

Values:
Love, Creativity,
Giving

Paulsen, Gary, *Hatchet*. Bradbury Press, 1987. (5–12) Newbery Honor
While fourteen-year-old Brian is on his way to spend the summer with his father in Canada, the small plane crashes. Brian is not seriously hurt, but must learn to survive alone in the wilderness, with only a hatchet to assist him. As he develops the resourcefulness to survive, he also learns to cope with the divorce of his parents.

Applications:
Language Arts–Compare to *My*
  Side of the Mountain
Science–Research plants and animals

Values:
Self-reliance, Courage,
Ingenuity

Peck, Richard, *Remembering the Good Times.* **Delacorte Press, 1985.** (9–12)

A compelling story of three young people who become inseparable friends at junior-high age and remain close until tragedy strikes and they are left with only the memories of the good times.

Applications:
Literature–Class discussion
Health–Coping with stress
Psychology–Dealing with grief,
   Single parenting

Values:
Friendship, Self-
   acceptance, Cross-
   generational rela-
   tionships

Pfeffer, Susan, *The Sebastian Sisters: Thea at Sixteen.* **Bantam, 1988 (9–12)**

Having recently purchasing their own house, the Sebastians are excited about redecorating and each of the four girls having a room of her own. The concerns of the family are rather shallow until Thea volunteers to work in a local hospital, where she beomes the Big Sister to a little girl who is dying of cancer.

Applications:
Health–Terminal illness
Literature–Creative writing,
   Journaling

Values:
Family unity,
Unselfishness,
Sacrifice, Compassion

Scott, Carol, *Kentucky Daughter.* **Clarion, 1985.** (9–12)

Mary Fred Pratley wants more from life than her coal mining town can supply. Her solution is to live with her aunt and uncle in Norfolk, Virginia, to have access to the advantages a larger school should offer. The challenges she meets are more than she expected. However, the values and courage she had learned in the hills of Kentucky assist her in gaining victory over problems she must face.

Applications:
Literature–Compare to *Lyddie* and
   Come Sing, Jimmy Jo
Psychology–Sexual harassment,
   Loneliness

Values:
Courage, Family unity,
Gifted children,
Friendship

Snyder, Carol, *The Leftover Kid.* **Pacer Books. 1986. (9–12)**
Wendy thinks that she finally has arrived at a wonderful age when her mother no longer hires an after school sitter for her. As Wendy is glorying in her new freedom, however, news comes that her sister, brother-in-law, and infant niece will be moving in with them temporarily. Then her maternal grandmother and paternal grandfather also take up residence in their home. With an infant in the house, Wendy's school project aimed at teaching adolescents the responsibilities of rearing a baby becomes all the more effective.

Applications:	Values:
Literature–Journaling, Compare life to Wendy's	Family unity, Taking responsibility,
Health–Girl's class	Cooperation

Sobol, Donald J., *Encyclopedia Brown Saves the Day.* **Illustrated by Leonard Shortall. Nelson, 1970. (4–7)**
Ten-year-old Leroy Brown, the son of the police chief, has earned the nickname of "Encyclopedia" by becoming a detective of some reputation in his small town of Idaville. Actually, Encyclopedia usually finds clues that assist his father in solutions. Readers may test their skills at crime fighting by predicting the guilty party. This is one of a continuing series.

Applications:	Values:
Language Arts–Creative writing, Prediction, Reading aloud, Reluctant readers	Observation, Analysis, Perseverance

Stoltz, Mary, *A Dog on Barkham Street.* **Harper, 1985. (2–8)**
Many children may relate to this story of wanting a dog before Mom thinks they are mature enough to care for a pet. This tale of Edward Frost and the dog who came for a visit concludes happily, but not without conflict and adventure.

Applications:	Values:
Language Arts–Recreational reading, Creative writing (Personal pet experiences)	Responsibility, Commitment, Dependability

Ure, Jean, *See You Thursday.* **Delacorte Press, 1981. (9–12)**
When Mrs. Fenton takes in a lodger, Marianne, her adolescent daughter, is less than delighted. When she finds out that he is blind, she is very resentful. Gradually, Marianne learns to accept Abe as he is. When she becomes too attached, her mother asks him to move out. Emphasis is laid on the normalcy of handicapped persons.

Applications:
Literature–Individual reading
Psychology–Handicapped people,
  Coping with first love

Values:
Celibacy,
Compassion,
Self-reliance

Voigt, Cynthia, *Dicey's Song.* **Atheneum, 1983. (9–12) Newbery Medal**
A sequel to *Homecoming,* this novel reveals the further development of the Tillerman children. Adjustment to a new environment, expression of individual identities, and learning to live with their newly found grandmother provide the elements of an award-winning plot.

Applications:
Literature–Characterization,
Psychology–Learning disabilities,
  Mental illness, Grieving,
  Gifted children

Values:
Family unity,
Cross-generational rela-
tionships, Friendship,
Self-acceptance

Voigt, Cynthia, *Homecoming.* **Atheneum, 1985. (9–12)**
Deserted by their mother in a Connecticut shopping mall, the four Tillerman children survive with scant money or directions. Led by indomitable thirteen-year-old Dicey, the children find the home of an aunt who takes them in out of obligation. Finding that to be an unacceptable situation, the little family heads to Maryland, where the only relative known to them is their enigmatic grandmother.

Applications:
Literature–Journaling
History–Trace trip on a map
Psychology–Desertion, Orphans

Values:
Family unity, Courage,
Love, Ingenuity

Voigt, Cynthia, *A Solitary Blue*. Fawcett Juniper/Ballantine, 1983. (9–12) Newbery Honor
As an eight-year-old, Jeff Greene is deserted by his mother. So begins the poignant pilgrimage of Jeff to accept himself, his father, and his mother's actions. The plot interweaves with *Dicey's Song* as Jeff and Dicey Tillerman help each other make sense of life.

Applications:	Values:
Psychology–Single parenting, Desertion	Father-son relationships, Forgiveness, Friendship, Self-acceptance

Warner, Gertrude Chandler, *The Boxcar Children*. Albert Whitman, 1977. (5–8)
Although the dialogue is reminiscent of early reading books, the multivolume series, of which this book is the first, has experienced a recent revival in popularity. First published in the 1940s, the storyline follows four orphans and a dog as they live for a time in a deserted train car. Adventure lightens the survival theme as the youngsters are independent yet cooperative, carrying out daily chores and other aspects of living on their own so they can stay together.

Applications:	Values:
Language Arts–Reluctant readers, Reading aloud, Compare to other orphan stories	Survival, Cooperation, Family unity, Courage

Wells, Rosemary, *The Man in the Woods*. Scholastic, 1984. (9–12)
Helen, a ninth-grader, believes that the wrong person has been incarcerated for a crime. When she tries to convince others, she is threatened by a mysterious man in the woods. With the help of her friend, Pinky, she finally sees justice served.

Applications:	Values:
Literature–Compare to other mysteries	Courage, Integrity, Friendship

Wells, Rosemary, *When No One Was Looking.* Dial Press, 1980. (9–12)

Everyone in her high school is convinced that Kathy Bardy has the potential to be a world-class tennis champion. Julia and Kathy have been friends since Kathy rescued Julia from an unpleasant situation back in their earliest school years. Both Julia's family, who are rich, and Kathy's family, who are not, are determined to work together to see that nothing will prevent Kathy from achieving the national stardom they feel she deserves. A new twist is added to the story when her chief competitor is found dead.

Applications:
Literature–Predicting, Creative
   writing
Psychology–Peer relationships,
   competition, Parent/child relationships, Stress
Sports–Tennis

Values:
Integrity, Self-
acceptance, Friendship

Williams, Barbara, *Beheaded, Survived.* Franklin Watts, 1987. (9–12)

Set in England, this near-formula-fiction focuses on the popular sibling and her plain sister who, in this case, is also diabetic. Jane (plain) and Courtney (older and popular) are part of a tour group of teenagers from America who are visiting places of literary interest. Jane is shy and only hopes that one of the six guys, or even a nice girl, will become her friend on the trip. Courtney, on the other hand, has snagged a rich fellow before the plane leaves American soil. Jane is also afraid of anyone discovering that she is diabetic. As she begins to take charge of her circumstances, she meets Lowell, who is himself dealing with severe emotional turmoil. The ending is satisfactory and the reader also learns something about the history of English literature.

Applications:
Psychology–Coping with grief
Health–Diabetes
Literature–British literature

Values:
Self-acceptance,
Friendship

Wood, June Rae, *The Man Who Loved Clowns*. Putnam, 1992. (5–12)

A tender yet unsentimental story of living with the mentally handicapped, this is one the reader will long remember. Several dimensions of love are explored as the teenaged protagonist shares life with her uncle who has Down's syndrome.

Applications: Values:

Literature–Individual reading   Individuality, Loyalty,

Health–Mental handicaps   Love, Survival

Psychology–Housing the mentally
  handicapped, Coping with grief

CHAPTER SEVEN

NONFICTION

When children ask for a book to read, the first response of an adult is often to hand them a storybook or a picture book without first finding out the child's interests or needs. The desire to learn is born in the heart of every child and some children (just as some adults), in their quest to find answers, prefer reading facts to reading fiction. These facts do not have to be boring, but can be presented in a way that creates a sense of awe and wonder in children, whetting their appetite for more information while satisfying   present curiosity.

Increasingly, nonfiction trade books are being used in classrooms to supplement and enhance textbook information. Ruth Heller's *How to Hide a Crocodile and Other Reptiles* uses rhyming text and excellent illustrations to teach primary students how crocodiles and other reptiles protect themselves through the use of camouflage. The detailed drawings of Edwin Tunis which accent his well-researched *Colonial Living* add much richness to a student's introduction to life in seventeenth-century America.

Children are also finding that nonfiction books provide a rich resource outside the classroom, answering questions about their hobbies. *The Victory Garden Kid's Book* (Waters) is an excellent resource for fledgling gardeners. Its illustrations are so clear that older children can read and follow the instructions on their own. If the pursuit is woodworking, Kevin McGuire has created an easy-to-read manual for the woodshop in his *Woodworking for Kids*. Just as adults turn to books to guide them through their problems, authors of children's materials attempt to help young people solve their own problems by writing about the things that touch their lives. One such series, entitled *What to Do When Your Mom Or Dad Says*. . . (Berry), presents guidance with parent/child relationships and skill development in areas related to communication, etiquette and grooming.

Although facts receive the heavy emphasis in nonfiction, narrative is often used to carry along the interest of the child so that the information being presented is more easily absorbed. *Flight: The Journey of Charles Lindburgh* (Burleigh) is presented in such vivid fashion that the reader is able to share the loneliness, danger, and final triumph that Lindburgh himself must have experienced in his flight across the English Channel. Cynthia Rylant tells about her native West Virginia with such charm in *Appalachia: The Voices of Sleeping Birds* that the reader senses the joy she felt in growing up in the mountains.

Through reading about the lives of people such as *Ben Carson* (Carson), who overcame the poverty of inner-city living to become a renowned neurosurgeon, or Elizabeth Blackwell, as described in *Dr. Elizabeth* (Clapp), who fought against prejudice and rejection to become the first woman doctor, young people can find inspiration to face everyday problems and to achieve the goals they have set.

Illustration for children's books has become an art form, and nowhere is it more important than in nonfiction books. Today's trade books for children are profusely illustrated and often pictures convey a majority of the information given. *Incredible Cross–Sections* by Stephen Biesty is an outstanding example of detailed, usually hidden information being made clear and simple to understand. *Muscles to Machines* (Ardley) combines drawings and photographs to create a profitable physics resource for home or school. Also, the whimsical pictures of Baskin in *Hosie's Zoo* and of Maurice Sendak in *A Hole Is to Dig* certainly make learning more fun.

Nonfiction is the fastest growing genre in children's literature, and with 60 to 70 percent of the books in most libraries being in this category, it is important to establish guidelines for their selection. Accuracy and currency of data given, as in *Volcano: The Eruption and Healing of Mount St. Helens* (Lauber), is of vital importance, with the author distinguishing between fact, theory and opinion. Clear structure, with chapters following in logical sequence as well as appropriate indexing, helps to give access to needed facts. Clarity and accuracy of illustration will also greatly enhance the value of the book. As in all books for children, a clear, understandable writing style with vocabulary appropriate for the target audience often determines whether the child will read further or lay the book down. Outstanding works of nonfiction convey the passions and convictions of the author in a way that reaches out and draws in the reader.

Because of the abundance of subject areas available, it is difficult to create a comprehensive list of nonfiction titles that all libraries should have on their shelves. We have attempted to present a list of outstanding titles on a variety of topics. Following the broad guidelines given for acquisition, this core collection could easily be expanded to meet the needs of the particular patrons being served.

American Heritage, editors, *Trappers and Mountain Men.* **American Heritage, 1961. (9–12)**
Using photographs and drawings from the time period portrayed, the editors depict the accomplishments of those who first ventured into the unknown territories of this continent. The title is one of a historical series about the development of the United States. Other titles in the series include *The Book of Indians, Clipper Ships and Captains, California Gold Rush,* and *Men of Science and Invention.*

Applications: Values:
History–United States,   Courage, Perseverance,
 Exploration   Individuality

Amery, Heather, and Katherine Folliot, *The First Thousand Words in French.* **Illustrated by Stephen Cartwright. Usborne Publishing, 1979. (K–4)**
With light-hearted illustrations and basic vocabulary, the authors have created a book for everyone who is trying to learn French. Included are a pronunciation guide and index to words in the pictures. Amery and Cartwright have also teamed up with other authors to create books which introduce English, German, and Spanish.

Applications: Values:
Language Arts–Language   Appreciation of other
 development   cultures
Social Studies–France

Ardley, Neil, *Muscles to Machines.* **Gloucester Press, 1990. (5–8)**
Readable print, clear illustrations, and well-chosen photographs make the books in the Hands-On-Science series a profitable resource in the classroom or at home. Each explanation includes a simple student project to demonstrate the principles being taught. This particular book deals with the fundamentals of energy and movement. Other books in the series include: *Wind and Flight, Rain to Dams, Rainbows to Lasers, Sound Waves and Music,* and *Magnets to Generators.*

Applications: Values:
Science–Projects with energy   Knowledge

Baskin, Leonard (illustrator) with words by Tobias, Hosea, Lucretia and Lisa Baskin and others, *Hosie's Zoo*. Viking Press, 1981. (K–4)
Baskin presents a zoo full of animals which are both familiar and obscure. His fantastic watercolors and the humorous, colorful descriptions give children a feel for the characters of the animals as well as a description of how they look.

Applications: Values:
Science–Animals   Love of animals
Art–Appreciation

Bennett, J. William, *The Book of Virtues*. Simon & Schuster, 1993. (4–12)
The underlying concept behind this treasury of moral stories, is that character matters. Bennett collected the many stories from the Bible, history, poetry, fables, philosophy, fiction, and fairy tales. This superb collection, arranged according to the virtues they represent, could be read aloud at bedtime, during class, or could be enjoyed by young readers alone.

Applications: Values:
Language Arts–Reading aloud   Self-discipline, Faith,
Bedtime stories   Compassion, Honesty,
                                 Perseverance, Courage,
                                 Loyalty, Responsibility

Biesty, Stephen (author and illustrator), *Incredible Cross–Sections*. Knopf Books for Young Readers, 1992. (4–12)
Incredible is an appropriate adjective to describe Stephen Biesty's book of cut-away illustrations, filled with information on how things work, how they were built, and how they are used. The reader is given a glimpse inside eighteen various buildings and machines.

Applications: Values:
Science–Physics   Knowledge
Art–Architecture
Use with *The Way Things Work*

Berry, Joy Wilt, *What to Do When Your Mom or Dad Says . . . Clean Yourself Up.* **Children's Press, 1982. (K–8)**
Commonsense directions are given to children who are sometimes confused by parent's demands. Although presented in a humorous, engaging way, the advice is thorough and sound.

Applications:	Values:
Language Arts–Communication	Obedience, Maturity,
Health–Etiquette, Grooming	Responsibility
Psychology–Parent/child	
relationships	

Burgess, Alan, *The Small Woman.* **Dutton, 1957. (5–12)**
Rejected by the China Inland Mission after a three-month probationary period at their training school in England, Gladys Aylward decides to go to China as a missionary on her own. The long, dangerous journey–and miraculous deliverances–foreshadow the flavor of her years in China. This moving story portrays China before the Communist regime.

Applications:	Values:
History–China	Unselfishness, Love,
Heroes	Perseverance,
Women	Dedication

Burleigh, Robert (author and illustrator), *Flight: the Journey of Charles Lindbergh.* **Illustrated by Mike Wimmer. Philomel, 1991. (K–4) Caldecott Honor**
At twenty-five years of age, Charles Lindbergh accomplished what many thought was impossible: flying non-stop from Long Island, New York, to Paris, France. Through Burleigh's dramatic prose and Wimmer's vivid paintings, the reader is able to share some of the loneliness, weariness, danger, and triumph of that historic flight.

Applications:	Values:
Language Arts–Compare to *The*	Courage, Determination
Wright Brothers by Charles Ludwig	
Science–Flight	

Burnie, David, *Tree*. Alfred A. Knopf, 1988 (5–12)
Pages filled with captioned photographs give an exceptionally clear presentation of the life cycle of trees. This book could be shared as a read-aloud for children or used as a reference by adults. Other titles in the *Eyewitness Book Series* include topics of historic and scientific interest, such as *Car, Bird, Money, Insect, Sports, Knights, Flying Machine, Arms and Armor, Fish, Rocks and Minerals, Mammal,* and *Flag.*

Applications:
Science–Trees, Inventions, Ecology

Values:
Respect for nature

Butterworth, Nick, and Mick Inkpen, *The Little Gate*. Zondervan, 1989. (K–4)
Delightful, humorous illustrations highlight this easy-reading version of the New Testament parable regarding the camel and the needle's eye. The book's small size makes it an easy fit for a child's hand. Other titles in the series include: *The House on the Rock, The Lost Sheep, The Rich Farmer,* and *The Good Stranger.*

Applications:
Language Arts–Parables

Values:
Humility, Humor, Faith

Carson, Ben, with Cecil Murphy, *Ben Carson*. Zondervan, 1992. (5–8)
Ben Carson, who is now director of pediatric neurosurgery at Johns Hopkins Hospital in Baltimore, Maryland, grew up in a poor inner-city environment. Determined to encourage her children to work for high goals in life, Ben's mother required them to read many books. This early training helped him to overcome obstacles in achieving his present status. Older readers might enjoy his autobiography *Gifted Hands.* This book is part of a series entitled *Today's Heroes.* Other persons covered in the series include Billy Graham, Colin Powell, and Joni Eareckson.

Applications:
Career exploration
Heroes

Values:
Faith, Diligence, Courage

Charlip, Remy, et al., *Handtalk: An ABC of Finger Spelling and Sign Language.* **Scholastic, 1974. (5–12)**
Communication involves more than speech. Eyes, face, and even hands can talk. In this book, Charlip offers an introduction to two methods of talking with one's hands: finger spelling and signing. The words, illustrated with double-spread photographs, are fun and simple to follow.

Applications:
Health–Deafness, Physical
  Handicaps

Values:
Communication, Under-
  standing of others'
  limitations

Clapp, Patricia, *Dr. Elizabeth.* **Lothrop, Lee and Shepard, 1974. (9–12)**
In her struggle to become the first woman doctor, Elizabeth Blackwell suffered much opposition and rejection, but she also led an exciting and challenging life. Through her courage and determination she did much to open the field of medicine to women.

Applications:
Health–Medicine
History–Victorian life, Women's
  studies

Values:
Courage, Determination

Corwin, Judith Hoffman (author and illustrator), *Colonial American Crafts: The Home.* **Franklin Watt, 1989. (5–8)**
Children will enjoy the five craft projects and eight recipes they can make while learning about the homes of Colonial America from 1607 to 1776. Projects include a friendship pillow and a treasure box. Two other titles in the series describe life in *The Village* and *The School.*

Applications:
History–American colonial life
Art–Primitive art, Painting
Applied Arts–Cooking,
  Sewing

Values:
Stewardship, Work
ethic

Daugherty, James (author and illustrator), *Daniel Boone.* **Viking Press, 1939. (5–8)**
Daugherty felt that a book artist should be a storyteller in picture and that illustrations should comment on character and humanity as well as physical appearance. His larger-than-life drawings enthusiastically convey the challenges, the joys, and the drama of the life of legendary Daniel Boone.

Applications:	Values:
Language Arts–Storytelling	Courage, Work ethic,
Social Studies–Frontier and pioneer life	Determination
Heroes	

D'Aulaire, Ingri and Edgar (authors and illustrators), *Abraham Lincoln.* **Doubleday, 1939, 1957. (K–4) Caldecott Medal**
Although Edgar was born in Germany and Ingri in Norway, the couple considered the United States their adopted nation. One of the great Americans they admired, Abraham Lincoln, became the subject of this book, which won the Caldecott Medal for 1940. With their books about famous American heroes, the D'Aulaires helped to establish picture books as an art form.

Applications:	Values:
Social Studies–Civil War, Frontier and pioneer life	Determination, Work ethic, Compassion
Heroes	

Devlin, Harry (author and illustrator), *To Grandfather's House We Go.* **Four Winds Press, 1967. (5–8)**
With colorful, photo-like drawings, Harry Devlin gives his readers a quick history of American architecture from 1664 to the late 1800s. From the log homes of the early settlers to Victorian eclectics, the author describes each one with affectionate detail.

Applications:	Values:
Art–Architecture	Appreciation of
History–United States	ancestors

Dingwall, Laima, and Annabel Slaight, ed., *Owl's Winter Fun.* Golden Press, 1984. (5–8)
This book is filled with interesting science activities, word games, puzzles, stories, and projects. Compiled by OWL magazine, it makes an excellent resource for parents and teachers. A similar collection is published for summer learning and entertainment.

Applications: Values:
Science–Experiments,   Creativity, Knowledge,
  Ecology   Experimentation

Foster, Genvieve (author and illustrator), *George Washington's World.* Charles Scribner's World, 1941. (5–8)
Genvieve Foster wrote only history or biographies, and *George Washington's World* was her first book. Since history was dull and confusing to her in school, she has made it readable and alive for others, showing what was going on around the world at each point in her subject's life. Her books would be excellent references for the whole language classroom.

Applications: Values:
History–Multicultural cross-   Unselfishness, Courage
  references, Research Washington
Heroes

Frank, Anne, *Diary of a Young Girl.* Pocket Books, 1990. (9–12)
During the two years that her family and friends spend hiding from the Nazis, Anne keeps a diary of her own adolescent confusions and the quarrels and misunderstanding brought about by their confinement. In spite of the hardships they endure, Anne remains hopeful for her future and is sensitive to other's feelings.

Applications: Values:
Language Arts–Compare to   Kindness, Compassion
  Number the Stars
History–World War II, Jews
Psychology–Coming of age

Freedman, Russell, *Lincoln, A Photobiography.* **Ticknor and Fields: Houghton Mifflin, 1987. (5–12) Newbery Medal**
This is a warm, readable biography of Abraham Lincoln. Beginning with his boyhood career as a lawyer and marriage to Mary Todd, the author focuses most attention on the presidential years. Freedman is able to explain in a clear manner the complex issues with which Lincoln struggled during the Civil War years.

Applications:	Values:
History–Civil War, Presidency, Elections	Humor, Work Ethic, Steadfastness,
Heroes	Passion for learning, Compassion

Gish, Duane T., *Dinosaurs: Those Terrible Lizards.* **Illustrated by Marvin Ross. Creation–Life, 1977. (K–8)**
Where did dinosaurs come from? What did they look like? Whatever became of the dinosaurs? Does the Bible mention dinosaurs? Backing his information with many years of research, Dr. Gish gives possible answers to these questions.

Applications:	Values:
Science–Dinosaurs, Research to compare and contrast with other books on the same topic	Knowledge

Gwynne, Fred (author and illustrator), *A Little Pigeon Toad.* **Simon and Schuster, 1988. (2–4)**
A little girl voices the confusion caused by the expressions her family has used. She wants to know if Uncle Walter really sews his fields, and if flowers have pistols. With colorful, humorous illustrations the author introduces children to the world of homonyms and commonly used idioms.

Applications:	Values:
Language Arts–Homonyms, Figurative Speech, Creative writing	Humor, Understanding

Hautzig, Esther, *At Home in Four Languages*. Illustrated by Aliki. Macmillan, 1968. (K–4)
Hautzig celebrates home and family in four languages in this whimsically illustrated book.   Using Chicago, Marseilles, Barcelona, and Leningrad as backdrops, she presents basic vocabulary of English, French, Spanish, and Russian which relate to everyday activities.

Applications:
Foreign Language–Basic
  vocabulary
Social Studies–Cultural awareness,
  Naming likeness and differences

Values:
Family unity, Communi-
cation

Hayes, Ann, *Meet the Orchestra*. Illustrated by Karmen Thompson. Harcourt Brace, 1991. (K–4)
Meet a rabbit with her flute and an alligator playing the drums. With Thompson's amusing full-page illustrations and the author's colorful descriptions of the way the instruments sound, children are enticed to learn more about the field of music.

Applications:
Music–Introduce musical
  instruments, Take field trip
  to hear an orchestra

Values:
Music appreciation
Humor

Heller, Ruth (author and illustrator), *How to Hide a Crocodile and Other Reptiles*. Grosset & Dunlap, 1986. (K–4)
This is one title in a series of small books by Heller designed to introduce science topics to young children. Her excellent artwork and rhyming text make the books a joy to read. Other subjects about which she has written are butterflies, gray tree frogs, polar bears, whippoorwills, and octopuses.

Applications:
Science–Camouflage, Reptiles
Art–Collage

Values:
Knowledge

Jenkins, Peter, *A Walk across America*, and *The Walk West*. Morrow, 1979, 1981. (9–12)
Searching for the true character of America, Peter Jenkins determined to walk from coast to coast, stopping to work when necessary and meeting as many people as possible. While in the South, he met and married Barbara, who continued the walk with him. Together they introduce the reader to touching, yet humorous stories of the people and the natural world of this continent. Peter's next walk, described in *A Walk Across China*, is just as captivatingly real.

Applications: Values:
History–Geography, China,   Determination,
  Cultural Awareness   Patriotism

Johnson, Gerald, *America Is Born*, *America Grows Up*, and *America Moves Forward*. Illustrated by Leonard Fisher. Morrow, 1959. (5–8) Newbery Honor
Enriched by the excellent pen and ink drawings of Leonard Fisher, this history series presents both major and less-familiar events that brought America from early to modern times. Its pages describe in understandable form not only the events, but also their underlying causes, so that with enlarged understanding of the past, readers can make wiser choices regarding the future.

Applications: Values:
Social Studies–United States,   Decision making
  Enrichment

Joslin, Sesyle, *What Do You Say Dear?* Illustrated by Maurice Sendak. Addison–Wesley, 1958. (K–4) Caldecott Honor
This humorous Caldecott Honor book uses exaggeration to introduce very young children to some basic manners. The same author and illustrator team continued their instruction to children in a second title, *What Do You Do Dear?*

Applications: Values:
Health–Etiquette, Role Playing   Politeness, Respect,
                                     Humor

Kherdian, David, *The Road from Home.* **Viking Penguin, 1979. (9–12) Newbery Honor.**
In 1915, the decision of the Turkish government to exterminate the Armenians living within their borders shatters the once-happy life of seven-year-old Veron. Sent on a death march through the desert, she survives starvation, an epidemic and the execution of family and friends. To keep herself alive, Veron (who would in time become Kherdian's mother), clings to her hope for a new life in far-off America.

Applications: Values:
History–Turkey, Armenians,   Perseverance, Courage
   Race relations
Survival Stories

Krauss, Ruth, *A Hole Is to Dig: A First Book of First Definitions.* **Illustrated by Maurice Sendak. Harper & Row, 1952. (K–4) Caldecott Honor**
In this first book of definitions, Krauss is able to define words in ways that have meaning for small children. The illustrations by Maurice Sendak are a delightful complement to the narrative.

Applications: Values:
Language Arts–Definition of   Humor, Knowledge
   words

Krementz, Jill (author and photographer), *A Very Young Skater.* **Alfred A. Knopf, 1979. (K–4)**
A well-known photographer and author, Krementz takes her readers into the fascinating professional worlds of ballet, horseback riding, gymnastics, the circus, and ice skating by describing the lives of children who are a part of them. Kathrine Healy, who began skating at age three, makes a winsome heroine in this title. Through the author's photographs the reader can join Katherine as she is learning, practicing, competing, and performing.

Applications: Values:
Career exploration   Determination, Courage,
Sports–Ice Skating   Responsibility

Kurelek, William (author and illustrator), *A Prairie Boy's Winter.* **Tundra Book, 1973.** (4–8)
Through his many paintings and spare prose, this renowned artist tells about growing up on the prairie through the economically hard days of the 1930s. In spite of the chores they had to do, he and his friends found time to play exciting games on the ice and in the snow. Equally engaging is his book *A Prairie Boy's Summer.*

Applications:
Social Studie–The Midwest,
The Great Depression
Language Arts–Compare to *Little House on the Prairie*

Values:
Dependability, Work ethic, Family love

Lane, Margaret, *The Tale of Beatrix Potter.* **Penguin, 1946.** (6–12)
Known to the world as the author of small picture books about animals, Potter was also a naturalist, artist, and thoroughgoing botanist. Late in life she married, gave up writing for children, and became a lady farmer. The means she developed for coping with a lonely childhood may bring comfort and courage to children who feel neglected. Young adults may find valuable answers to survival in the life of this famous woman.

Applications:
Language Arts–Biography
History–England

Values:
Coping with loneliness

Lauber, Patricia, *Volcano: The Eruption and Healing of Mount St. Helens.* **Aladdin, 1986.** (5–12)
Newbery Honor
In 1980, Mount St. Helens exploded in the largest volcanic eruption in United States history. Scientists who witnessed the event share their awe at the power of the volcano and the resilience of life in its aftermath. Seventy-five color photographs document the event.

Applications:
Science–Volcanoes, Methods of scientific observation

Values:
Knowledge, Appreciation of nature

Lindvall, Ella K., *Read-Aloud Bible Stories.* **Illustrated by H. Kent Puckett. Moody Press, 1982. (K–4)**
Even the youngest child can understand these Bible stories that use a minimum of words and a maximum of picture. This volume was awarded the Gold Medallion Book Award and was named a C. S. Lewis Honor Book.

Applications:	Values:
Language Arts–Role playing, Bible stories	Knowledge of the Bible

Ludwig, Charles, *The Wright Brothers.* **(The Sower series) Mott Media, 1985. (5–12)**
From their youth, the Wright brothers showed creativity and determination. Encouraged by their parents, the boys earned money to buy tools and parts to build numerous machines. As men, their determination and cooperation allowed them to accomplish what others said could never be done.

Applications:	Values:
Science–Flight, Inventions	Ingenuity, Family
Language Arts–Compare to other biographies of Wright brothers	unity, Determination
Psychology–Self-acceptance	

Macaulay, David (author and illustrator), *Ship.* **Houghton Mifflin, 1993. (5–12)**
Modern underwater archaeologists search for a sunken caravel in the reefs of the Caribbean. As the artifacts are recovered, clues to the birth of the ship are revealed. Macaulay presents a wealth of historical and technological information through engaging narrative and excellent illustrations. The author's book *Castles* won a Caldecott honor book award in 1978 and is now available on video.

Applications:	Values:
Archaeology–Underwater	Courage,
Science–Ships	Precision
History–15th Century	

McGuire, Kevin, *Woodworking for Kids.* **Sterling, 1993. (4–8)**
Illustrated with close-up, full-color photographs, this book makes an extremely clear, easy-to-read manual for putting together simple woodworking projects. Each activity is identified by skill level and comes with a materials list and safety tips. Designs include a wooden tool box, a bike rack, a bird box, adjustable stilts, a puppet theater, and more.

Applications:
Applied Arts–Woodworking skills
Mathematics–Measurement

Values:
Self-reliance, Patience,
Precision

McKissack, Patricia, *The Apache.* **Children's Press, 1984. (K–4)**
In this small, profusely illustrated book, both student and teacher can learn a great deal about the Apache Indians. McKissack begins with the location of the earliest tribes and gives the semantic background to the name of the tribe. The final chapter, entitled "The Apache Today," explains what customs are still adhered to, what tribespeople are doing as vocations, and how their philosophy of life has enabled them to survive.

Applications:
Social Studies–Native Americans
Art–Research arts and crafts

Values:
Appreciation of other
cultures

McKissack, Patricia, *Martin Luther King, Jr.: A Man To Remember.* **Regensteiner Publishing Enterprises, 1984. (5–8)**
Beginning with King's birth, including some not-so-widely known facts regarding his naming, and concluding with an allusion to a biblical quote, the author stresses the human side of this black leader. The author asserts that King never gave up because of his faith in God. This is a book that would give children of color hope to continue to work for the betterment of their race without bitterness.

Applications:
Language Arts–Biography
Social Studies–Race relations

Values:
Faith, Courage,
Leadership

Parker, Steve, *The Body Atlas.* **Illustrated by Giuliano Fornari. Doring Kindersley, 1993.** (9–12)
Steve Parker has created a comprehensive visual guide to the human body. Detailed, accurate illustrations allow the reader to see what happens to food after it is swallowed and how the heart pumps blood through the body. Use in conjunction with *The Human Body Pop-Up Book* published by Penguin.

Applications: Values:
Science–Anatomy, Research   Knowledge
Health–Unit on care of the body

Petry, Ann, *Harriet Tubman: Conductor on the Underground Railroad.* **Crowell, 1955.** (5–10)
Not content to gain her own freedom from bondage, Harriet Tubman returned to the South again and again, putting herself at great risk, to eventually lead more than three hundred slaves to safety in the North. This biography depicts the hardships that slaves endured living on plantations and it reveals the inner workings of the Underground Railroad.

Applications: Values:
History–Civil War, Underground   Courage, Self-sacrifice
  Railroad, Slavery, Research
  Tubman, Black History Month

Provensen, Alice and Martin (authors and illustrators), *The Glorious Flight.* **Puffin Books, 1983.** (K–4) **Caldecott Medal**
With wit and humor, the Provensens convey the excitement, dangers, and frustrations experienced by Louis Bleriot, who gave his life and his fortune as a pioneer of aviation. In 1909 "Bleriot XI" became the first airplane to fly across the English Channel.

Applications: Values:
Science–Flight   Inventiveness,
Social Studies–France   Perseverance
Heroes–Compare with *The*
  Wright Brothers

Raboff, Ernest, *Leonardo Da Vinci.* Doubleday, 1971. (5–8)
Part of a series called "Art for Children," this book presents the work of one of the finest artists of all time. The author uses a light approach, vocabulary understandable to the young, and includes a brief biographical sketch along with fifteen reproductions of Da Vinci's work. Other artists covered in the series include Renoir, Michelangelo, Rembrandt, and Rousseau.

Applications:
Art–Da Vinci
Language Arts–Biographies

Values:
Patience, Self-control,
Dedication to learning

Rylant, Cynthia, *Appalachia: The Voices of Sleeping Birds.* Illustrated by Barry Moser. Harcourt Brace Jovanovich, 1991. (K–4) Caldecott Honor
The poetic prose of Cynthia Rylant combined with the photo-like illustrations of Barry Moser re-create the lifestyle of the Appalachian mountain area. The tone throughout is one of warmth and love and an appreciation for the people who live in the region.

Applications:
Social Studies–Geography
Language Arts–Use with *When I
  Was Young in the Mountains*
  and *The Relatives Came*

Values:
Family unity, Cultural
appreciation,
Steadfastness

Spier, Peter (author and illustrator), *Noah's Ark.* Doubleday, 1977. (K–4) Caldecott Medal
With rhyming text, Spier introduces the familiar story with his own translation of a seventeenth-century Dutch poem, "The Flood." The rest of the book is a refreshing wordless depiction of life on the ark during the great rain. Animals of all kinds parade across the pages with Noah and his family as they escape the deep waters to emerge again on dry land.

Applications:
Language Arts–Easy reading,
  Storytelling, Bible stories

Values:
Faith, Imagination
Hard work, Love

Tada, Joni Eareckson, *Joni.* **Bantam, 1976. (9–12)**
After breaking her neck in a diving accident at age seventeen, Joni found that her arms and legs were paralyzed for life. Overwhelmed at first by her handicap, Joni found strength to face life through the support of her faith, her family, and friends. Since then she has gone on to become an accomplished author, an artist, a singer, and a public speaker. In all that Joni does, she conveys a message of hope and encouragement to others.

Applications: Values:
Health–Physical handicaps   Courage, Determination
Psychology–Survival   Family unity

Terban, Marvin, *Mad as a Wet Hen: And Other Funny Idioms.* **Illustrated by Guiliuo Maestro. Clarion Books, 1987. (5–8)**
Marvin Rerban explains the meanings of over one hundred idioms in this book, which is humorously illustrated by Guilio Maestro. It is the third book in the series Word Play Books, published by Clarion.

Applications: Values:
Language Arts–Idioms   Humor, Information
Health–ESL or deaf children

Thigpen, Thomas Paul, *Stories in the Sky.* **Illustrated by Dennis Jones. David C. Cook, 1986. (5–8)**
Star patterns have been named by many different cultures in various ways. This title recognizes Bible stories in these configurations, while giving the reader a wealth of historical and scientific information about the stars. Constellations named include Jonah's Great Fish, Noah's Ark, The Coat of Many Colors, and Goliath.

Applications: Values:
Science–Astronomy,   Knowledge
    Take field trip to an observatory
Language Arts–Bible stories,
    Collect or write poems relating
    to sun, moon and stars
Art–Mosaic, Collage

Tunis, Edwin (author and illustrator), *Colonial Living.*
Thomas Crowell, 1957. (9–12)
The detailed pen and ink drawings scattered liberally throughout the
well-researched text give an excellent introduction to life in
seventeenth-century America. Any of these historical works by
Tunis would be a beneficial addition to a collection: *Frontier
Living, Weapons, Wheels.*

Applications: Values:
History–United States,   Knowledge, Diligence,
  Colonial period   Craftsmanship

Van Cleave, Janice, *Physics for Every Kid.* **Illustrated by
Barbara Clark. John Wiley and Sons, 1991.** (7–12)
Janice Van Cleave teaches students that science is fun, stimulating
their desire to know more about various science disciplines. This
book includes 101 physics experiments that can be done with
materials that are easily accessible around the house. The
experiments are safe and they work. Other books in the series
describe experiments in astronomy, biology, chemistry, earth
science, and gravity.

Applications: Values:
Science–Experiments   Knowledge,
                                          Curiosity

Waters, Marjorie, *The Victory Garden Kid's Book.*
Houghton Mifflin, 1988. (3–12)
For the adult who wants to make children excited about gardening,
this is an excellent resource. Older children will be able to read for
themselves the clear step-by-step instructions that begin with
buying needed materials and end with harvesting crops. Younger
children can follow the seventy-five photos and seventy drawings
with the guidance of an adult.

Applications: Values:
Science–Conservation   Nature appreciation,
Health–Nutrition   Responsibility,
Practical Arts–Gardening   Stewardship

Yates, Elizabeth, *Amos Fortune, Free Man.* **E. P. Dutton, 1950.** **(5–8) Newbery Award**
Born an African prince, At-Mun was captured by traders, brought to Boston, and sold to a Quaker family as a slave. He was treated well, but his heart yearned for freedom. At age sixty, he purchased his own freedom and immediately began to save for the purchase price of another. Integrity, faith, hard work, and compassion characterized the life of Amos Fortune.

Applications: Values:
History–United States–Colonial   Work ethic, Love,
   period, Black history, Slavery   Self-sacrifice,
Language Arts–Dramatization   Integrity

CHAPTER EIGHT
POETRY

When I recently asked college students in a children's literature class to define poetry, one insightful coed wrote, "Poetry is you–on paper." Though this statement may be a generalization, it embodies the essence of that special form of literature. Poetry cuts away all that is unnecessary and leaves what the writer sees as the reality of his life. Well-written poetry leaves the reader or listener changed a bit, inspiring insight, increasing compassion, creating a desire to be more tolerant of those who are different, or giving birth to a sense of delight.

The child who develops the ability to express himself in verse usually is prompted by exposure to the writings of others who have won acclaim in the genre. As with other categories of children's literature, there is indeed a veritable feast of verse available. Historically, we still have reprint upon reprint of A. A. Milne's whimsical poems. His works have innocent appeal for the young child, yet enough worldly wisdom for the adult seeking comfort from the burdens of life. His books *When We Were Young* and *Now We Are Six* have enjoyed more than half a century of popularity and continue to bring delight to each new generation fortunate enough to share their charm. Contemporary writer Valerie Worth has produced one small volume with almost infinite possibilities. Her compilation of four books, *All The Small Poems*, exalts the simple things in life such as water buckets, porches, and garden hoses. Clever pen and ink illustrations by Natalie Babbitt accompany the verses and thus form a perfect partnership in tribute to items often overlooked as subjects of poetic praise.

Single poem volumes, such as Longfellow's *Hiawatha*, are shown to their best advantage in picture book format through the craft of talented artists such as Susan Jeffers. Listeners too young to understand the text will certainly remember the haunting loveliness of Jeffers's art long after the story is over. The older reader will revel in both.

Nancy Larrick, Lee Bennett Hopkins, and others have made great contributions to the field of children's literature by compiling samples of the best poetry for young readers. Whether following a specific theme as in *On City Streets*, or simply stockpiling good poetry as in *Piping Down the Valleys Wild*, Larrick has shared a great legacy. *Side by Side*, compiled by Hopkins and energized by Hilary Knight's illustrations of romping children, demonstrates that even the most active young person can still enjoy well-chosen verse.

Finally, we include a variety of Mother Goose versions, each bearing a unique feature. Since these familiar rhymes provide a child's first exposure to the literary world, we wanted to offer somewhat of a cross section of available collections. From the rebus format of *The Real Mother Goose Picture Word Rhymes,* to the classic illustrations of the Jessie Wilcox Smith reprinting, we encourage you to reminisce as you share with your young person those lines which first introduced you to the magic world of Mother Goose.

Poetry reaches out to both the head and the heart. We challenge you, the adult, to have an unquenchable thirst for a variety of verse and we believe that both your life and that of your special child will be enriched as a result. We hope

as you share these selections we have suggested that you and
the child reader/listener will also experiment with allowing
your emotions to escape and discover the joy of finding
yourself–on paper.

Andersen, Hans Christian (adapted by Jon Erickson), *The Woman with the Eggs.* **Illustrated by Jan Mogensen. Gareth Stevens, 1987. (K–4)**
A single poem with humorous illustrations comprises this excellent demonstration of what happens when one counts chickens before they hatch. The moral is made clear without being didactic.
Applications:
Language Arts–Reading aloud,
  Memorization, Introduction to the
  works of Hans Christian Andersen

Bierhorst, John (editor), *In the Trail of the Wind.* **Doubleday, 1971. (5–12)**
In his collection of poem and other ritual orations, Bierhorst gives the reader a glimpse into the essence of many tribes of Native Americans, as well as the Eskimo. A brief factual introduction makes the text even more meaningful.
Applications:
Social Studies–Native Americans
Language Arts–Creative writing
Art–Native American designs

Boone, Debby, *Bedtime Hugs for Little Ones.* **Illustrated by Gabriel Ferrer. Harvest House, 1988. (K–4)**
This "warm and fuzzy" collection of poems is certain to lend security to the young child when it is time to tuck in for the evening. Written by singer and actress Debby Boone and illustrated by her husband, both text and pictures carry a sense of home, hearth, and heart through childlike drawings and common activity, like bathing, counting sheep, and hugging.
Applications:
Language Arts–Reading aloud,
  Dramatization, Memorization,
  Bedtime stories

Checkerboard Press (compiler), *The Real Mother Goose Picture Word Rhymes.* **Illustrated by Blanche Fisher Wright. Macmillan, 1916, 1944, 1987. (K–4)**
The unique feature of this collection is the rebus format illustrating each verse. Beginning readers may use the key at the bottom of each page to learn new words from the pictures given.
Applications:
Language Arts–Reading aloud,
    Choral reading, Beginning reading
    Building sight vocabulary, Dramatization
Math–Counting

Coatsworth, Elizabeth, *The Sparrow Bush.* **Illustrated by Stefan Martin. W. W. North, 1966. (K–8)**
Sixty-two small works of art grace the pages of this volume of verse. Coatsworth's focus is mainly on nature and the general experiences of a pleasant childhood in the country.
Applications:
Language Arts–Choral reading,
    Creative writing,
    Poetry
Art–Inspiration from nature
Science – Nature

Cole, William, *A Zooful of Animals.* **Illustrated by Lynn Munsinger. Houghton Mifflin, 1992. (K–4)**
Cole and Munsinger have created the perfect match of illustration and poetry in this bright, light trip to the zoo. Contributors include Kipling, Aldis, Ciardi, and many others. Topics range from wise to zany.
Applications:
Language Arts–Reading aloud,
    Dramatization,
    Choral reading
Art–Appreciation of talent

Cole, William (compiler), *Poem Stew.* **Illustrated by Karen Ann Weinhaus. J. B. Lippincott, 1981. (K–8)**
Incorporating both well-known authors and those not famous, Cole compiles a menu with many entrees. Each poem focuses on food or some aspect of eating. From the thanksgiving turkey to a gnat swallowed accidently, servings are humorous and in good taste.
Applications:
Language Arts–Reading aloud
Health–Foods (cooking, serving, manners)

Craig, Jean (compiler), *The Sand, the Sea and Me.* **Illustrated by Newell Audrey. Walker and Company, 1972. (K–8)**
Watercolor illustrations in shades of the sea complement this collection for the child who loves to vacation on the beach, lives there, or who has never been. Craig has compiled vignettes in verse that will entice readers to stick their toes in the sand.
Applications:
Psychology–Overcoming fear of the ocean
Science–Nature study,
   Sea life

De Gasztold, Carmen (translated by Rumer Godden), *Prayers from the Ark.* **Illustrated by Jean Primrose. Penguin Books, 1986. (K–12)**
Actually, the title is self–explanatory. DeGasztold has spoken for the animals and left her readers with what she thinks the animal, bird, or insect might have said to God. Each reveals the personality, temperament, or spirit that we humans would see as realistic for the creature.
Applications:
Language Arts–Reading aloud,
   Creative writing
Science–Research animals
Art–Make collage of animals

de Regniers, Beatrice and others (compilers), *Sing a Song of Popcorn.* **Scholastic Hardcover, 1988. (K–8)**
Impressive is the word for this combination of poetry and pictures. The list of contributors reads like a Hall of Fame in children's literature. Caldecott Medal–winning artists like Arnold Lobel, Maurice Sendak, and Trina Schart Hyman supply the illustrations for poets both contemporary and classic. Variety and quality would aptly describe this volume.
Applications:
Language Arts–Reading aloud, Memorization
Art–Appreciation
Health–Humor

Fisher, Aileen, *Feathered Ones and Furry.* **Illustrated by Eric Carle. Thomas Y. Crowell, 1971. (K–8)**
Although this volume contains only thirty-seven pages, each page contains several entries. Habitat, seasonal changes, life cycles as well as respect for wildlife are reflected in the writings of this well-known poet. Carle's linoleum cuts, all black on tan and white paper, express the essence of each creature portrayed in verse.
Applications:
Language Arts–Reading aloud
Science–Research animals
Art–Create potato cuts

Fisher, Aileen, *Runny Days, Sunny Days.* **Abelard-Schuman, 1958. (K–4)**
To sample the poems in this collection is to peek inside the child's mind and glimpse his perception of nature. Seasons, holidays, animals, and insects all parade through the pages and the reader is delighted to follow.
Applications:
Language Arts–Reading aloud
Science–Nature
Health–Humor

Frost, Robert, *Birches*. Illustrated by Ed Young. Henry Holt, 1988. (5–12)
Ed Young has joined hands with Robert Frost to achieve a masterpiece of both lyric and line. Broken down into two, three, or four lines per page and made almost concrete by Young's illustrations, this narrative poem will be enjoyed by all ages.
Applications:
Language Arts–Reading aloud
Art–Appreciation
Science–Trees

Frost, Robert, *You Come Too*. Holt, Rinehart and Winston, 1964. (5–12)
The title of this small volume of poetry especially selected for young people is an invitation by the writer to share his world. The reader is transported to New England farm country to view life from Frost's unique rural philosophy.
Applications:
Language Arts–Reading aloud, Creative writing
Social Studies–Rural life

Grover, Eulalie Osgood, *The Classic Volland Edition Mother Goose*. Illustrated by Fredrick Richardson. Rand McNally, 1985. (K–3)
After a lengthy and informative introduction regarding the legend of Mother Goose, Osgood presents the adult reader and the small listener with a comprehensive selection of the rhymes that first made the enigmatic Grandmother of children's literature a household word. This oversize book, with its authentic illustra–tions, gives a delicious taste of the era when children and adults first sampled Peter's pumpkin, Contrary Mary's garden, and Hot Cross Buns.
Applications:
Language Arts–Poetry
Music–Singing tunes, movement and clapping

Hayes, Sarah, and Toni Goffe, *Clap Your Hands: Finger Rhymes.* **Lothrop, Lee & Shephard, 1988. (K–4)**
For the very youngest listener, this collection of finger plays will provide a happy introduction to poetry. Traditional and contemporary rhymes are included, with illustrations of charming little folk demonstrating just what the adult should do to add life to each verse.
Applications:
Language Arts–Finger plays,
  Memorization, Dramatization

Hirschfelder, Arlene B., and Beverly Singer (compilers), *Rising Voices: Writings of Young Native Americans.* **Macmillan, 1992. (8–12)**
If Americans with European ancestry and Judeo-Christian religious heritage are to understand the Native Americans upon whose land they settled, then poetry may serve as a doorway to such knowledge. This collection of poems and essays reflects the expression of Indian youth as they write about their life, families, rituals, and beliefs.
Applications:
Language Arts–Creative writing
History–Native Americans
Religion–Comparison of beliefs

Hopkins, Lee Bennett (compiler), *Pterodactyls and Pizza.* **Trumpet Book Club, 1992. (K–8)**
A contemporary collection of poems about everyday life, with which the modern child can readily identify, fills this volume. Some are brief enough to memorize for fun with one or two readings. Subjects include people, places, animals, nature, and humor.
Applications:
Language Arts–Reading aloud, Memorization,
  Dramatization
Health–Humor
Science–Nature

Hopkins, Lee Bennett (collector), *Side by Side: Poems to Read Together.* **Illustrated by Hilary Knight. Simon and Schuster, 1988.** (K–4)
At the conclusion of this versatile collection, Hopkins and Knight each add a personal note on the influence of poetry in their own lives. Variety and energy characterize the contents of this book that begs to be shared. Contemporary and traditional writers alike are included. Knight's illustrations invite lingering and smiling over each page.
Applications:
Language Arts–Reading aloud
Health–Humor
Science–Nature, Seasons

Hughes, Langston (selected by Lee Bennett Hopkins), *Don't You Turn Back: Poems.* **Illustrated by Ann Grifalconi. Alfred A. Knopf, 1969.** (K–12)
Such a sensitively beautiful collection of this great African-American poet's work is difficult to capture in annotation. For any library, this is a must, especially as a read-aloud source.
Applications:
Art–Collage
Social Studies–Black history
Psychology–Self–acceptance, Motivation

Jacobs, Leland, *Poetry for Bird Watchers.* **Garrard Publishing, 1970.** (5–8)
Chapters include bird watching, sounds, songs, and thoughts about the feathered ones. This small volume reveals fact and encourages fantasy for the avian observer. Variety in poetic form and vocabulary makes this a good resource for the elementary-school child.
Applications:
Language Arts–Reading aloud
Art–Collage
Science–Birds, Nature

Jeffers, Susan (illustrator and compiler), *Mother Goose: If Wishes Were Horses and Other Rhymes.* **Puffin Unicorn, 1979. (K–12)**
Children, adults, horses, and dogs romp through the pages of this small book with such energy and beauty that the reader will be drawn back again and again by both the traditional text and the joyful illustrations.
Applications:
Language Arts–Reading aloud
Arts–Movement, Humor, Perspective

Johnson, James Weldon, *The Creation.* **Illustrated by James E. Ransome. Holiday House, 1994. (K–12)**
Johnson's narrative account of Creation is illuminated by full-page and border illustrations that reflect the power of the subject. Accompanying the primary theme are smaller paintings of an old Black storyteller, relating the account to a group of children whose expressions change in response to the mood of the events related. A work of art in text and illustration.
Applications:
Language Arts–Reading aloud, Reader's theater
Art–Mural of events
Social Studies–Black History Month

Kennedy, X. J., *The Beasts of Bethlehem.* **Illustrated by Michael McCurdy. Macmillan, 1992. (K–8)**
According to legend, on Christmas Eve all animals may speak in language understandable by man. Kennedy has opened the stable door in Bethlehem so that the reader may hear what might have been said on that first holy night. From the proud hawk to the humble beetle, voices fit the speaker. A delightful addition to the traditional Christmas collection.
Applications:
Language Arts–Dramatization, Memorization
Art–Mural

Kuskin, Karla, *The Rose on My Cake.* Harper and Row, 1964. (K–4)
Kuskin has captured the child's viewpoint in this slim volume. Insight may be gained by parents as they read how children perceive daily occurrences, such as feeling they are doing nothing right, as well as what's wrong with birthday parties (the title poem). Both adults and children will enjoy the humor and candid voice in this book.
Applications:
Language Arts–Reading aloud, Creative writing
Mathematics–Counting

Larrick, Nancy, *Bring Me All Your Dreams.* Evans and Company, 1980. (K–12)
How dull life would be without dreams–sometimes even hopeless. Such must have been the inspiration for this collection which contains a wide variety of poems crossing centuries and cultures. Special features include brief biographical sketches of contributors at the end of the book.
Applications:
Language Arts–Reading aloud, Creative writing
   about dreams, ambitions, wishes

Larrick, Nancy, *On City Streets.* Evans and Company, 1968. (5–12)
Nancy Larrick enlisted the young people who are most familiar with the "music" of the streets to help make selections for this volume of urban poetry, resulting in images with which the city child will identify and the country child will find compelling. The hardback version is illustrated with photographs from the sixties, and may appear dated, but the ideas are timeless.
Applications:
Language Arts–Creative writing
Social Studies–City life, Family life,
Art–Collage of urban items

Larrick, Nancy (compiler), *Piping Down the Valleys Wild.* **Dell, 1968. (K–12)**
Poetry that appeals to a variety of ages, tastes and styles is found in this collection. Both classic writers, such as Robert Louis Stevenson, and contemporary ones, such as Karla Kuskin, are included. Containing old favorites and those that promise to become the same, this volume is a must for any collection.
Applications:
Language Arts–Reading aloud, Dramatization
Health–Humor

Lewis, Claudia, *Long Ago in Oregon.* **Illustrated by Joel Fontaine. Harper and Row, 1987. (4–8)**
The title says it all except that this small volume is quite introspective, and written from the point of view of a child. Lewis reports that she has been writing since she was ten years old, and the observations and responses to life in the Northwest in the early nineteen hundreds is reflected in candid blank verse appropriate to that age. Family life, vignettes of neighbors, growing up, moving, and, of course, picnics are enhanced by the soft black-and-white illustrations.
Applications:
Language Arts–Creative writing, Poetry
Social Studies–World War I, Family life
Art–Pen and ink

Lobel, Arnold (author and illustrator), *Pigericks.* **Harper & Row, 1983. (K–8)**
As might be guessed from the title, this is a humorous collection of limericks focusing on pigs. Lobel is sure to win the heart of the most nonpoetic reader with his amusing verses and lively illustrations.
Applications:
Language Arts–Introduction to writing poetry, Reading aloud
Art–Create original illustrations
Science–Research pigs

Lobel, Arnold (compiler and illustrator), *The Random House Book of Mother Goose.* **Random House, 1986. (K–3)**
Lobel has chosen 306 nursery rhymes to include and illustrate in his award-winning style. Because of its quantity as well as its quality, this collection will add its own special significance to a library shelf. Illustration and text strike a perfect match.
Applications:
Language Arts–Reading aloud, Rhyming,
   Dramatization, Rhythm

Longfellow, Henry Wadsworth, *Hiawatha.* **Illustrated by Susan Jeffers. Dial Books, 1983. (5–8)**
Jeffers has chosen a favorite section of the lengthy narrative poem to form her text. Illustrations are detailed and sensitively sympathetic to the Native American culture. Although the poetic language may be difficult for children, meaning will be clear through the illustration.
Applications:
Language Arts–Narrative poetry
Social Studies–Native Americans
Art–Appreciation

Lucas, Barbara (compiler), *Little People's Mother Goose.* **Illustrated by Jeni Bassett, Derrydale Books, 1988. (K–3)**
Large book format and lots of open space with animals acting out the rhymes in animated fashion will make this book of old familiar rhymes enjoyable for the small listener. Koalas, kangaroos, and other exotic animals join the more common sheep and cows in dramatizing each rhyme.
Applications:
Language Arts–Reading aloud, Introduction to rhyme,
   Dramatization, Memorization
Math–Counting

McCord, David, *Take Sky*. Little, Brown & Company, 1961. (K–12)
The title poem of this small book reflects McCord's purpose in writing verses for the young and the young at heart. He demonstrates how simple words and everyday objects provide excellent inspiration for writing. He does not propose that writing is effortless, but rather rewarding and creative.
Applications:
Language Arts–Reading aloud, Choral reading,
   Introduction to writing poetry
Psychology–Creative therapy

Merriam, Eve, *Blackberry Ink*. Illustrated by Hans Wilhelm. William Morrow & Co., 1985. (K–4)
This little volume contains rollicking repetitious verse that the younger child will love to hear and repeat. For the youngest listeners and beginning readers there are poems to entertain and amuse. Everyday activities, and fantastic happenings, serve as subjects for Merriam's lighthearted lines.
Applications:
Language Art–Reading aloud, Introduction to poetry
Art–Illustrate the poems
Psychology–Humor

Milne, A. A., *When We Were Very Young*. E.P. Dutton, 1924. (K–12)
In the introduction, Milne explains the ageless appeal of his verses. Some will suit the young child quite well, while the adult will find others memorable, and perhaps reminiscent of his own childhood. Everyday occurrences, etiquette, friendship, holidays, and much more are fuel for the poetic fire in this very special volume.
Applications:
Language Arts–Introduction to poetry,
   Reading aloud, Dramatization
Social Studies–Compare British lifestyle with American

O'Neill, Mary, *Hailstones and Halibut Bones.* **Doubleday, 1961. (K–4)**
Color is the central theme of this slim volume. Each page focuses on one element of the spectrum, calling the reader's attention to items that share the same shade. All the senses are invited along as O'Neill shares the smell, taste, and feel of colors.
Applications:
Language Arts–Reading aloud
Science–Prism and color wheel
Art–Creative use of one color

Silverstein, Shel, *Where the Sidewalk Ends.* **Harper Collins, 1974. (K–12)**
For more than twenty years, the author and illustrator of this volume of poetry has been considered the voice of the child. Adults may be horrified at some of his bizarre creations, but there is no doubt that many children who otherwise would find poetry to be quite dull have responded with enthusiasm to the verses contained in this work and its companion, *A Light in the Attic.*
Applications:
Language Arts–Reading aloud, Dramatization,
   Introduction to poetry
Psychology–Humor

Smith, Jessie Willcox (compiler and illustrator), *Mother Goose.* **Derrydale Books, 1986. (K–4)**
This comprehensive collection of more than 600 Mother Goose rhymes expresses in verse many facets of life at the turn of the century. Smith's love of children is reflected in her tender illustrations in both color and black and white.
Applications:
Language Arts–Reading aloud, Memorization,
   Introduction to poetry

Stevenson, Robert Louis, *A Child's Garden of Verses.*
**Illustrated by Alice and Martin Provensen. Simon and
Schuster, 1951.** **(K–12)**
The value and popularity of this classic is verified by the fact that
new editions are still being published, and that other well-known
illustrators such as Tasha Tudor, Jessie Wilcox Smith, and Brian
Wildsmith have chosen to illustrate earlier versions. Many adults
first loved poetry as a result of having been read Stevenson's
Verses. No library should be without it.
Applications:
Language Arts–Reading aloud, Memorization
Social Studies–Victorian life

Thayer, Ernest Lawrence, *Casey at the Bat.* **Illustrated
by Ken Bachaus. Raintree Publishers, 1985.** **(4–12)**
With the sports-participation, sports-enthusiasm, perhaps sports-
worship which exists in many modern lifestyles, this classic poem
in picture book format helps keep the heroes of the game in
perspective. Expressive illustrations depicting period uniforms take
the reader right to the ballpark. A great edition for any library.
Applications:
Language Arts–Poetry for sports fans,
   Dramatization, Reading aloud

Tudor, Tasha (collector and illustrator), *Wings from the
Wind.* **J. B. Lippincott, 1964.** **(K–8)**
This small volume is packed with lovely poetry and illustrations
alike. Tudor has collected some of the best classic poems from
Shakespeare, Coatsworth, the Song of Solomon, and Emily
Dickinson. Divisions of poetry include Thoughts, As the Earth
Turns, Birds of the Air, Beasts of the Field, and Nonsense.
Applications:
Language Arts–Listening, Writing
Science–Nature
Social Studies–Holidays, History

Untermeyer, Louis (compiler), *The Golden Treasury of Poetry.* **Illustrated by Joan Walsh Anglund. Golden Press, 1959.** **(K–12)**
If the number of printings is any indication of the popularity of this work, it is well worth the investment. By 1966 it was in its ninth printing. With 316 large pages crammed with stories and poems covering topics from Creation through nonsense verse, this lavishly illustrated volume is a necessity for the poetry collection.
Applications:
Language Arts–Reading aloud, Memorization
Psychology–Humor
Science–Seasons, Months

Untermeyer, Louis (compiler), *Rainbow in the Sky.* **Harcourt, Brace & World, 1963.** **(K–12)**
This comprehensive volume has a range of interest, type and difficulty that reaches all age levels, and includes some poems which are international in content. Authors include Robert Burns, Edward Lear, Edgar Allen Poe, and David McCord.
Applications:
Language Arts–Memorization, Creative writing
Social Studies–Folklore of many countries

Worth, Valerie, *All the Small Poems.* **Illustrated by Natalie Babbitt.** **Farrar, Straus and Giroux, 1987.** **(K–12)**
A collection of all the poems which this NCTE Award winner has written that fall within the category of "small poems" is a treasure for anyone who enjoys seeing common things in an uncommon way. Worth writes about subjects ranging from rags to jewels and earthworms to dinosaurs, frequently with profound insight.
Applications:
Language Arts–Reading aloud, Creative writing
Art–Line drawings

Wright, Blanche Fisher (collector and illustrator), *The Real Mother Goose Picture Word Rhymes.* **Rand McNally and Co., 1916, 1944. (K–4)**
Since the preschool child is often eager to read as a mark of maturity, this edition of the old favorite is especially appealing. Blanche Wright has employed rebus writing to enable the young ones to read by using identifiable pictures. A glossary of illustrations is given at the bottom of each large, colorfully illustrated page.

Applications:
Language Arts – Reading aloud, Beginning reader,
 Introduction to Poetry

RECOMMENDED AUTHORS

Inclusion in the regular body of this core collection indicates an endorsement of a particular title, not necessarily the life work of an author. In the following list, we would like to recognize authors who consistently delight, instruct, and entertain their readers and whose volumes can be used to introduce children to literature that promotes the development of positive values in their lives. Some of these authors consistently win awards and others are excellent writers whose works are never chosen by the committees who make these momentous decisions, but we believe that reading any one of their stories would be a valuable activity.

Alcott, Louisa May
Anno, Mitsumasa
Atwater, Richard
Baum, L. Frank
Berry, Joy
Blair, Walter
Bond, Michael
Brink, Carol Ryrie
Brown, Marc
Brown, Margaret Wise
Bulla, Clyde Robert
Bunn, T. Davis
Burnett, Frances Hodgson

Byars, Betsy
Carle, Eric
Caudill, Rebecca
Chase, Richard
Cleary, Beverly
Cleaver, Vera and Bill
Coatsworth, Elizabeth
Cooper, James Fenimore
Crews, Donald
D'Aulaire, Ingri and
    Edgar
Daugherty, James
Davoll, Barbara

DeAngeli, Marguerite
DeJong, Meindert
dePaola, Tomie
Dickens, Charles
Doyle, Sir Arthur Conan
Edmonds, Walter D.
Enright, Elizabeth
Fields, Rachel
Fisher, Aileen
Freedman, Russell
Fritz, Jean
Frost, Robert
Gag, Wanda
Garfield, Leon
George, Jean Craighead
Giff, Patricia R.
Harris, Joel Chandler
Henry, Marguerite
Hoban, Russell
Hopkins, Lee Bennett
Hughes, Langston
Hunt, Angela Elwell
Jackson, Dave and Nita
Jacques, Brian
Johnson, James Weldon
Keats, Ezra Jack
Kellogg, Steven
Kennedy, X. J.
Kjelgaard, Jim
Kraus, Robert
Lang, Andrews
Larrick, Nancy
Lawhead, Stephen
Lawson, Robert

Lenski, Lois
Leppard, Lois Gladys
Lewis, C. S.
Lionni, Leo
Lofting, Hugh
Longfellow, Henry W.
Lucado, Max
MacDonald, George,
Mains, David and Karen
Marshall, Catherine
McCloskey, Robert
McCord, David
McDaniel Lurlene
McKissack, Patricia
Milne, A. A.
Montgomery, L. M.
Morris, Gilbert
Norton, Mary
O'Dell, Scott
Oke, Janette
Paterson, Katherine
Pella, Judith
Phillips, Michael
Polacco, Patricia
Porter, Gene Stratton
Potter, Beatrix
Pyle, Howard
Say, Allen
Scarry, Richard
Scott, Sir Walter
Speare, Elizabeth George
Young, Ed
Zemach, Harve
Zolotow, Charlotte

AWARD WINNERS

Throughout this collection, you will have noted the mention of awards won by particular books under discussion. Not all honors are listed because we felt that, in some cases, there were so many that to show all would be counter– productive and cumbersome. We did note each winner of the coveted Newbery or Caldecott Medals, or Honor books of the same distinction. We chose those because they are the ones most often referred to by teachers, librarians, and paperback book clubs and are featured on displays in book stores, and therefore are of special interest to the adult who wishes to be informed.

In this appendix, we will give a brief description of selected awards given both to books and to authors or illustrators. We have chosen just a few from the many possible categories to give you an idea of the variety of honors designed to enhance the quality of writing for children, both in our country and abroad. It is encouraging to see such interest in the standards of literature for children and young adults.

As with any award, not everyone will agree with all the choices. We do not necessarily recommend all books that win recognition, but we want our readers to be informed and to draw their own conclusions. It seems to us that books that are chosen to receive honors are often a reflection of current events. Children's books often act as a mirror to reflect the spirit of the time, and the spirit may not be the one you wish to instill in your young person. However, children who do not know about the world may not be as well equipped to deal with the future.

The other consideration to bear in mind when reading award books is that all those we have listed were chosen by adults. They may not necessarily be the ones children would select. There are other lists, and probably lists of lists, that note children's choices. You may want to consult one or more lists if the child with whom you are in touch is a reluctant reader.

We do think that award books have been selected over others for a reason and therefore deserve a look, a read, or perhaps several readings. We hope that the vast array of honor books will be helpful in the selection of titles to share with your young person.

NEWBERY AWARD

The Newbery Award was named for John Newbery, an eighteenth-century British publisher who had the courage to take the financial risk of printing books that would entertain children, as well as instructing them. He was a pioneer in the field of children's books and is well deserving of the award given in his honor. The American Library Association gives this award annually to the book chosen as the most distinguished children's book published in the United States the previous year. Emphasis is placed on text, not on illustration. This award has been given annually since 1922. The first award was received by Hendrick van Loon for *The Story of Mankind.*

Other books that might be thought of as runners-up have the distinction of being Honor books. All winners of the Newbery Award and Honor books included in this collection are noted in individual entries.

NEWBERY WINNERS

1922 van Loon, Hendrik Willem, *The Story of Mankind*
1923 Lofting, Hugh, *The Voyages of Doctor Dolittle*
1924 Hawes, Charles, *The Dark Frigate*
1925 Finger, Charles, *Tales from Silver Lands*
1926 Chrisman, Arthur Bowie, *Shen of the Sea*
1927 James, Will, *Smoky the Cowhorse*
1928 Mukerji, Dhan Gopal, *Gay-neck, The Story of a Pigeon*
1929 Kelly, Eric P., *The Trumpeter of Krakow*
1930 Field, Rachel, *Hitty: Her First Hundred Years*
1931 Coatsworth, Elizabeth, *The Cat Who Went to Heaven*
1932 Armer, Laura Adams, *Waterless Mountain*
1933 Lewis, Elizabeth Foreman, *Young Fu of the Upper Yangtze*
1934 Meigs, Cornelia, *Invincible Louisa: The Story of the Author of* Little Women
1935 Shannon, Monica, *Dobry*
1936 Brink, Carol Ryrie, *Caddie Woodlawn*
1937 Sawyer, Ruth, *Roller Skates*
1938 Seredy, Kate, *The White Stag*
1939 Enright, Elizabeth, *Thimble Summer*
1940 Daugherty, James, *Daniel Boone*
1941 Sperry, Armstrong, *Call It Courage*
1942 Edmonds, Walter D., *The Matchlock Gun*
1943 Gray, Elizabeth Jane, *Adam of the Road*
1944 Forbes, Esther, *Johnny Tremain*

1945   Lawson, Robert, *Rabbit Hill*
1946   Lenski, Lois, *Strawberry Girl*
1947   Bailey, Carolyn Sherwin, *Miss Hickory*
1948   duBois, William Pene, *The Twenty-One Balloons*
1949   Henry, Marguerite, *King of the Wind*
1950   deAngeli, Marguerite, *The Door in the Wall*
1951   Yates, Elizabeth, *Amos Fortune, Free Man*
1952   Estes, Eleanor, *Ginger Pye*
1953   Clark, Ann Nolan, *Secret of the Andes*
1954   Krumgold, Joseph, *. . .And Now Miguel*
1955   DeJong, Meindert, *The Wheel on the School*
1956   Latham, Jean Lee, *Carry On, Mr. Bowditch*
1957   Sorensen, Virginia, *Miracles on Maple Hill*
1958   Keith, Harold, *Rifles for Watie*
1959   Speare, Elizabeth George, *The Witch of Blackbird Pond*
1960   Krumgold, Joseph, *Onion John*
1961   O'Dell, Scott, *Island of the Blue Dolphins*
1962   Speare, Elizabeth George, *The Bronze Bow*
1963   L'Engle, Madeleine, *A Wrinkle in Time*
1964   Neville, Emily Cheney, *It 's Like This, Cat*
1965   Wojciechowska, Maia, *Shadow of a Bull*
1966   de Trevino, Elizabeth Borten, *I, Juan de Paraja*
1967   Hunt, Irene, *Up a Road Slowly*
1968   Konigsburg, E. L., *From the Mixed-Up Files of Mrs. Basil E. Frankweiler*
1969   Alexander, Lloyd, *The High King*
1970   Armstrong, William H., *Sounder*
1971   Byars, Betsy, *Summer of the Swans*
1972   O'Brien, Robert C., *Mrs. Frisby and the Rats of NIMH*
1973   George, Jean Craighead, *Julie of the Wolves*
1974   Fox, Paula, *The Slave Dancer*
1975   Hamilton, Virginia, *M. C. Higgins, the Great*

1976   Cooper, Susan, *The Grey King*
1977   Taylor, Mildred D., *Roll of Thunder, Hear My Cry*
1978   Paterson, Katherine, *Bridge to Terabithia*
1979   Raskin, Ellen, *The Westing Game*
1980   Blos, Joan, *A Gathering of Days: A New England Girl's Journal 1830–32*
1981   Paterson, Katherine, *Jacob Have I Loved*
1982   Willard, Nancy, *A Visit to William Blake's Inn*
1983   Voigt, Cynthia, *Dicey's Song*
1984   Cleary, Beverly, *Dear Mr. Henshaw*
1985   McKinley, Robin, *The Hero and the Crown*
1986   MacLachlan, Patricia, *Sarah, Plain and Tall*
1987   Fleischman, Sid, *The Whipping Boy*
1988   Freedman, Russell, *Lincoln: A Photobiography*
1989   Fleischman, Paul, *Joyful Noise: Poems for Two Voices*
1990   Lowry, Lois, *Number the Stars*
1991   Spinelli, Jerry, *Maniac Magee*
1992   Naylor, Phillis Reynolds, *Shiloh*
1993   Rylant, Cynthia, *Missing May*
1994   Lowry, Lois, *The Giver*
1995   Creech, Sharon, *Walk Two Moons*
1996   Cushman, Karen, *The Midwife's Apprentice*

CALDECOTT AWARD

The American Library Association has chosen to honor illustrators of children's books with an annual award begun in 1938. It was named for Randolph Caldecott, an eighteenth-century illustrator of books for young people. He was chosen because of his style of art which is often described as "lively." Compared to the masterpieces available in the twentieth century, his work is not remarkable, but his is the spirit that is still desired today. The Caldecott Medal and Honor winners must have been published in the United States during the year prior to the award, and are judged for illustration, although the story line certainly must also be acceptable. Dorothy P. Lathrop was the first winner for *Animals of the Bible*, written by Helen Dean Fish.

CALDECOTT WINNERS

1938   Fish, Helen Dean, *Animals of the Bible*. Illustrated by Dorothy P. Lathrop

1939   Handforth, Thomas, *Mei Li*

1940   d'Aulaire, Ingri and Edgar, *Abraham Lincoln*

1941   Lawson, Robert, *They Were Strong and Good*

1942   McCloskey, Robert, *Make Way for Ducklings*

1943   Burton, Virginia Lee, *The Little House*

1944   Thurber, James, *Many Moons*. Illustrated by Louis Slobodkin

1945   Field, Rachel, *Prayer for a Child*. Illustrated by Elizabeth Orton Jones

1946   Petersham, Maud and Miska, *The Rooster Crows*

1947   MacDonald, Golden, *The Little Island*. Illustrated by Leonard Weisgard

1948   Tresselt, Alvin, *White Snow, Bright Snow*. Illustrated by Roger Duvoisin

1949   Hader, Berta and Elmer, *The Big Snow*

1950   Politi, Leo, *Song of the Swallows*

1951   Milhous, Katherine, *The Egg Tree*

1952   Lipking, William, *Finders Keepers*. Illustrated by Nicolas Mordvinoff

1953   Ward, Lynd, *The Biggest Bear*

1954   Bemelmans, Ludwig, *Madeline's Rescue*

1955   Perrault, Charles, *Cinderella, or the Little Glass Slipper*. Illustrated by Marcia Brown

1956 Langstaff, John, *Frog Went Acourtin'*. Illustrated by Feodor Rojonkovsky

1957 Udry, Janice May, *A Tree Is Nice*

1958 McCloskey, Robert, *Time of Wonder*

1959 Cooney, Barbara, *Chanticleer and the Fox*

1960 Ets, Marie Hall, *Nine Days to Christmas*

1961 Robbins, Ruth, *Baboushka and the Three Kings*. Illustrated by Nicolas Sidjakov

1962 Brown, Marcia, *Once a Mouse* . . .

1963 Keats, Ezra Jack, *The Snowy Day*

1964 Sendak, Maurice, *Where the Wild Things Are*

1965 deRegniers, Beatrick Schenk, *May I Bring a Friend?* Illustrated by Beni Montresor

1966 Leodhas, Sorche Nic, *Always Room for One More*. Illustrated by Nonny Hogrogian

1967 Ness, Evaline, *Sam, Bangs & Moonshine*

1968 Emberley, Barbara, *Drummer Hoff*. Illustrated by Ed Emberley

1969 Ransome, Arthur, *The Fool of the World and the Flying Ship*. Illustrated by Uri Shulevitz

1970 Steig, William, *Sylvester and the Magic Pebble*

1971 Haley, Gail E., *A Story–A Story: An African Tale*

1972 Hogrogian, Nonny, *One Fine Day*

1973 Mosel, Arlene, *The Funny Woman*. Illustrated by Blair Lent

1974 Zemach, Harve, *Duffy and the Devil*. Illustrated by Margot Zemach

1975 McDermott, Gerald, *Arrow to the Sun*

1976 Aardema, Verna, *Why Mosquitos Buzz in People's Ears*. Illustrated by Leo and Diane Dillon

1977 Musgrove, Margaret, *Ashanti to Zulu: African Traditions*. Illustrated by Leo and Diane Dillon

1978 Spier, Peter, *Noah's Ark*

1979 Goble, Paul, *The Girl Who Loved Wild Horses*

1980   Hall, Donald, *Ox-Cart Man.* Illustrated by Barbara
        Cooney
1981   Lobel, Arnold, *Fables*
1982   Van Allsburg, Chris, *Jumanji*
1983   Cendrars, Blaise, *Shadow.* Illustrated by Marcia
        Brown
1984   Provenson, Alice and Martin, *The Glorious Flight:
        Across the Channel with Louis Bleriot July 25, 1909*
1985   Hodges, Margaret, *Saint George and the Dragon.*
        Illustrated by Trina Schart Hyman
1986   Van Allsburg, Chris, *The Polar Express*
1987   Yorinks, Arthur, *Hey Al.* Illustrated by Richard
        Egielski
1988   Yolen, Jane, *Owl Moon.* Illustrated by John
        Schoenherr
1989   Ackerman, Karen, *Song and Dance Man.*
        Illustrated by Stephen Gammell
1990   Young, Ed, *Lon Po Po: A Red-Riding Hood Story
        from China*
1991   Macaulay, David, *Black and White*
1992   Wiesner, David, *Tuesday*
1993   McCully, Emily Arnold, *Mirette on the High Wire*
1994   Say, Allen, *Grandfather's Journey*
1995   Bunting, Eve, *Smokey Night.* Illustrated by David
        Diaz
1996   Rathman, Peggy, *Officer Buckle and Gloria*

HANS CHRISTIAN ANDERSEN AWARD

This international award, given in honor of the revered storyteller for whom it is named, is awarded every two years by the International Board on Books for Young People. Originally presented to authors but expanded in 1966 to include illustrators, the Andersen award recognizes creators whose complete works are worthy of note. Eleanor Farjeon from Great Britain was the first recipient in 1956. Winners from the United States include Meindert DeJong (1962), Maurice Sendak (1970), Scott O'Dell (1972), Paula Fox (1978), and Virginia Hamilton (1992).

MILDRED L. BATCHELDER AWARD

This award is given annually by the American Library Association for the most outstanding children's book translated from the original language of publication into English the previous year. *The Little Man,* written by Erich Kastner and translated by James Kirup, was the first recipient of this honor in 1967.

CARNEGIE MEDAL

This award is given to the author of a book considered the most outstanding by the British Library Association. It has been awarded annually since 1937. To qualify, the book must have been first published in English within the United Kingdom during the previous year. The first recipient was Arthur Ransome for *Pigeon Post.*

THE KATE GREENWAY MEDAL

Awarded by the British Library Association annually since 1956, the recipient of this honor is recognized for outstanding illustration of a children's book published in the United Kingdom during the preceding year. Edward Ardizzone was the first to be presented with the medal for *Tim All Alone,* which he both wrote and illustrated.

BOSTON GLOBE–HORN BOOK AWARD

In 1967, two highly respected publications, the *Boston Globe* and the *Horn Book Magazine,* joined in creating two prizes for excellence in children's books–one for text, the other for illustration. Nine years later, more specific categories were chosen: Outstanding Fiction or Poetry, Outstanding Nonfiction, and Outstanding Illustration. The first to win these awards were Erik Hauggard for text in *The Little Fishes* and Peter Spier for illustration in *London Bridge Is Falling Down.*

LAURA INGALLS WILDER AWARD

Named for the author of the beloved Little House series, this award is granted by the Association for Library Service to Children of the American Library Association. It is given to an author or illustrator for significant and consistent quality of contributions to the field of children's literature. It may be thought of as a lifetime achievement award. At its inception in 1954, the award was given every five years. Since 1980, it has been awarded every three years. Laura Ingalls Wilder herself was the first recipient.

CORETTA SCOTT KING AWARD

Established by the American Library Association in 1970 to commemorate the dedication of both Martin Luther King, Jr., and his wife, for whom the award is named, this award is given annually to both a black author and illustrator. The criteria for winning this award include creating a work which encourages world unity and peace while serving as an inspiration to young people to achieve their goals. Lillie Patterson was the first recipient for *Martin Luther King Jr.: Man of Peace.*

NATIONAL COUNCIL OF TEACHERS OF ENGLISH AWARD FOR EXCELLENCE IN POETRY

Originally awarded every year, this award is given in recognition of significant contributions in writing poetry. Established by the awarding body designated in the title (NCTE), it recognizes the whole body of work published by living authors. Since 1982, it has been given every three years. David McCord was the first to be awarded this honor.

SCOTT O'DELL AWARD

To promote excellence in the writing of historical fiction, the prolific and highly respected author for whom this recognition was named established this award in 1984. His criteria included literary merit, as well as accurate research. The story must be set in the New World and be published in English by a United States company. The first to win the award was Elizabeth George Speare for *The Sign of the Beaver,* which is included in this collection.

THE JEFFERSON CUP

This award honors quality writing in the genres of biography, historical fiction, or American history. The author must be living in the Untied States, and the work published the year prior to the award. This recognition was created by the Virginia Library Association and is awarded by that body's Children's and Young Adult Round Table. The award has been given annually since 1983. Milton Meltzer was the first winner with *The Jewish Americans: A History in Their Own Words.*

SUBJECT INDEX

abuse, 116, 120, 136, 148
adoption, 118, 120
adolescence, 114
Africa, 10, 17, 22, 34, 53, 79, 84
African/Americans, 16, 43, 44, 74, 76, 82, 83, 86-89, 93, 94, 126, 148, 163, 173, 174, 178, 188, 189
aging, 147
alphabet, 9, 12, 15, 17, 79, 119
Amish, 78, 89
anatomy, 174
Ancient world, 104
animals, 6, 7, 9, 13, 17, 18, 22, 28, 61, 62, 64, 67, 75, 93, 119, 139, 161, 184, 185, 192
kindness to, 19
care of, 26
habitats, 28, 121
Appalachia, 39, 40, 91, 103, 122
archaeology, 172
architecture, 161, 165
Arctic life, 58
Armenia, 170
art
appreciation of, 9, 19, 28, 34, 45, 46, 48, 114, 161, 173, 175, 182, 183, 185, 186
collage, 11, 16, 35, 66, 69, 168, 176, 184, 188
drawing, 59, 62, 88, 89, 136, 164, 189, 196
origami, 35
astronomy, 176
Australia, 79
Austria, 5
awards, 201-210

baseball, 80, 195
bears, 9, 20, 26
bedtime stories, 4, 6, 14, 18, 19, 28, 162, 182
Bible stories, 172, 175, 176
biography, 171, 173, 175
birds, 28, 93, 188
birthdays, 6, 13, 14
Boston Globe-Horn Book Award, 210
Caldecott Award, 205-208
Cambodia, 77
Cameroon, 34
camouflage, 168
camping, 27
Canada, 117, 144
careers, 163, 170
Carnegie Medal, 209
cats, 12
chickens, 21
China, 53, 54, 78, 79, 84, 162, 169
Chinese/American, 87
chivalry, 123
choral reading, 183
Christmas, 5, 7, 13, 23, 41, 110, 150
Cinderella stories, 40, 53
cities, 82, 190
collage, 11
colonial life, 100, 108, 111, 164, 177, 178
colors, 8, 9, 21, 28, 81, 194
coming of age, 166
commitment, 112, 115, 152
communication, 16, 135, 140, 162, 164, 168

farm life, 8, 18, 21, 69, 78, 108,
114, 115, 127, 186
fear, 16, 25, 86, 92
figurative language, 149, 167
finger plays, 187
flight, 61, 162, 172, 174
Florida, 84, 121
fog, 25
folklore, 35, 43, 45, 196
football, 137
forests, 7, 27, 124
forgiveness, 23, 54, 81, 101, 114,
122, 148, 154
foster parents, 76
France, 63, 86, 107, 123, 139, 160,
174
Franklin, Benjamin, 63
freedom, 58, 112
French, 168
French Revolution, 106, 119
friendship, 11-13, 18, 20-21, 24,
47, 60, 61, 63-70, 75, 76, 86-89,
100, 116, 117, 124-126, 136,
138, 139, 141, 144, 145, 147,
149, 151, 154, 155
frogs, 20, 27
frontier life, 46, 101, 102, 107,
110, 111, 115, 118-120, 124,
125, 165
gardening, 22, 177
genealogy, 76, 91
generosity, 7, 14, 18, 22, 35, 110,
119
geography, 28, 169, 175
Germany, 45
gifted children, 64, 106, 107, 151,
153
giving, 7, 41, 48, 49, 82, 105, 150
government, 61, 65, 67, 109
grandparents, 4
gratitude, 22
grieving, 149, 151, 153, 156
grooming, 162
Hans Christian Andersen Award,
208-209
helpfulness, 23, 91
herbs, 103

heritage, 82, 88, 91, 92, 146, 165
heroes, 37, 46, 90, 162, 163, 165,
167
Hispanic, 44, 76, 77
history - 15th century, 172
holidays, 49, 195
Holland, 41, 78, 106, 123
homelessness, 86, 110, 135
homesickness, 92, 150
honesty, 8, 16, 21, 34, 47, 58, 84,
99, 101, 110, 135, 148, 161
honor, 38, 41, 44, 93, 114
hope, 76
horses, 140, 142, 143
humility, 12, 21, 39, 45, 48, 50,
66, 68, 102, 107, 109, 117, 163
humor, 4, 6, 9, 13-15, 17, 20, 23-
26, 34, 36, 37, 39, 42-44, 46,
52, 58-61, 64-70, 75, 86, 91,
109, 116, 123 127, 133, 137,
138, 141, 144, 149, 163, 167-
170, 176, 185, 187-189, 191,
193, 194, 196
ice skating, 170
illness, 134, 147, 151
imagination, 15, 21, 43, 46, 51, 60,
65, 70, 99, 175
immigration, 74, 76, 77, 81, 91, 93,
101, 112
independence, 39, 85
Indians of North America, 36, 41,
51, 74, 76, 81, 88, 90, 104, 110,
114, 120, 124, 125, 139, 173,
182, 187, 192
individuality, 13, 17, 18, 23, 29,
50, 54, 58, 77, 95, 134, 149,
156, 160
ingenuity, 12, 44, 52, 54, 61, 63,
64, 75, 78, 88, 92, 100, 102,
103, 116, 117, 119, 124, 125,
133, 135, 148, 150, 153, 172
initiative, 86
inquisitiveness, 12
insects, 8
integrity, 64, 83, 90, 113, 115, 118,
121, 145, 148, 154, 155, 178
inventiveness, 61, 163, 172, 174

stewardship, 177
storms, 10, 20, 21, 24
storytelling, 20, 34-38, 40-44, 48,
  49, 50, 51, 66, 86, 105, 165,
  173
stress, 155
suicide, 136, 137, 149
survival, 43, 66, 80, 84, 88, 92,
  102, 103, 111, 112, 121, 123,
  126, 133, 141, 145, 150, 154,
  156, 170 , 176
swans, 35
Sweden, 54
symbolism, 45, 53, 58, 64, 104
team spirit, 4, 64, 133
tennis, 155
Texas, 41
thankfulness, 11, 21, 26, 117
Thanksgiving, 77, 119
Thirty Years' War, 123
thoughtfulness, 65
tolerance, 68, 84, 90
traditions, 4, 28
transportation, 9, 13, 22, 23
trees, 163, 186
trickster tales, 34, 42
trust, 66, 140
Turkey, 170
Underground Railroad, The, 94,
  174
understanding, 85
U.S. history, 165, 169, 177
U.S. history - French and Indian
  War, 104

U.S. history - Revolutionary War,
  63, 107, 109
U.S. history - Civil War, 89, 99,
  100, 104, 113, 114, 122, 165,
  167
U.S. history - 1850-1900, 114,
  118, 120-122
unselfishness, 9, 20, 35, 46, 64,
  87, 108, 109, 114, 124, 134,
  151, 162, 166
Vermont, 111
Victorian era, 44, 99, 101, 113,
  115, 195
Virginia, 142
volcanoes, 171
vocabulary, 21, 23, 183
war, 77
weather, 10, 16, 20, 21, 24, 27, 51
wildlife, 13, 27, 140, 142
wind, 10
Wisconsin, 113
wisdom, 25, 34, 42, 43, 47, 50
wit, 100
woodworking, 173
work ethic, 7, 14, 36, 74, 94, 100,
  108, 121, 127, 164, 167, 171,
  178
World War I, 126, 191
World War II, 75, 78, 80-82, 85,
  112, 116, 117, 123, 125, 126,
  166
wordless books, 10, 13
Wyoming, 110

AUTHOR AND
TITLE INDEX

ABOUT THE AUTHORS

Janice DeLong holds two masters degrees in education, as well as having completed postgraduate hours in children's literature. She taught in both public and parochial schools for thirteen years before entering the collegiate system in 1985. She has served on the faculty at Liberty University in Lynchburg, Virginia, since that time. As a frequent speaker at workshops and supervisor of student teachers, she has had ample opportunity to hear the concerns of both teachers and administrators regarding the need to integrate literature with other content area subjects. From these experiences has sprung the format for *Core Collection for Small Libraries*.

Rachel Schwedt holds a master's degree in library science and has been a kindergarten teacher, an English teacher, and a librarian in both private and public schools. She presently supervises the curriculum and audio-visual libraries at Liberty University in Lynchburg Virginia. It was through her contacts with librarians and administrators in the private sector that she became aware of the need for an annotated collections list that librarians could use as a guideline in building their collections. Thus came the original impetus for developing *Core Collection for Small Libraries*.